AF652107

Buddhism in Nepal

Buddhism in Nepal

Sushil K. Naidu

KALINGA PUBLICATIONS
DELHI
2008

Rs. 550.00
$ 50.00
£ 25.00

First Published 2008
© Author
ISBN 978-81-87644-79-8

Published by
Rajat Sood
KALINGA PUBLICATIONS
10A, Pocket-I, Phase-I, Mayur Vihar, Delhi-110 091
Phone : 9810333246

Sole Distributor
MOHIT BOOK INTERNATIONAL
Publisher & Distributor
4649/21, Ansari Road, Darya Ganj, New Delhi-110 002
Phone : 011-23255141, Fax : 23280611
email: mohit_publication@rediffmail.com

PRINTED IN INDIA

Contents

Preface

Buddhist influences are evident in the culture of Nepal, Tibetan, Buddhism is the most widely practiced form. Many Buddhist groups are influenced by Hinduism in Nepal. Some ethnic groups in central Nepal are also followers of Buddhism.

This book aims at tracing the influences of Buddhism on this otherwise pre-dominantly Hindu Kingdom. Fact remains that the founder of Buddhism was born in Nepal. How in such a country only 11% of Nepal's population practice Buddhism?

Effort here is made to make available to our readers authoritative accounts of this fast expanding religion of the world on the country in, which its founder took birth. Attempt is also made to detail the history of Buddhism in Nepal.

Experts on the subject, Librarians and their staff members are respectfully acknowledge.

All praise to my publisher who is making all out efforts for wider publication of this profoundly important religion whose propagation is likely to bring peace to this terror sticken world of ours.

Sushil K. Naidu

1

Nepal - Ancient Buddhist Land

Nepal is an independent kingdom that lies 500 miles along the Himalayas. It is surrounded by Tibet and India. Nepal is divided into three sections: the northern snow mountains, the middle region, and the southern terai. Nepal has almost 20 million people and a variety of ethnic group. Most people speak Nepali and some speak English. Indo-Aryan immigrants originally settled Nepal in the 7th century B.C. Many tribes succeeded one another, until the Malla period, when three kingdoms were created: Kathmandu, Patan, and Bhaktapar. Recently a system of parliamentary democracy was established.

Buddhism in Nepal

Buddhism in Nepal dates from the birth of Siddharta Gautama himself. Legend has it that many bodhisattvas and previous Buddhas also visited the land. Monuments to these Buddhas can be seen. Early Buddhist history is difficult to document, but we know that Nepal became a great meeting point for Indian and Tibetan Buddhist teachers. Nagarjuna, the great Madhyamika mass and many other great practitioners visited, lived, and taught in Nepal. Stone inscriptions and colophons provide clear evidence that a strong lineage of Mahasanghika Bhiksunis existed in the seventh century. The country became a repository of Buddhist Sanskrit literature and famous for its production of fine Buddhist art.

Buddha Statue on Steps of Swayambunath Stupa, Kathmandu Valley.

Many famous temples have been erected throughout Nepal. Although many ancient temples was destroyed by earthquakes in 1355 and 1934, many important religious structures still survie. The ancient stupas of Swayambhu and Bodhnath are regarded as most sacred. Buddhism in Nepal includes Theravada, Mahayana and

Vajrayana traditions. The rulers of Nepal have primarily be Hindu, but have supported the development of Buddhism over the centuries. The Tibetan Mahayana tradition is the most popular in northern Nepal, with approximately 3000 monasteries Newar Vajrayana Buddhism is a widespread religious system in the Kathmandu Valley with an elaborate tradition of ritual. Since the early 40s some Nepalese have turned to Theravada practice based on the Pali canon, stressing the rational aspects of Buddhism over ritual. Most Theravada monasteries are located in the Kathmandu Valley. There are approximately 100 monks and 15 nuns, mostly belonging to the Newar community. Newars with the Shakya surname trace their lineage to the family of Shakyamuni Buddha.

The Great Stupa of Svayambhunath stands on a hill to the west of Kathmandu. Its name means "The self created, Self-existent Buddha." The myth of its origin is also the myth of the valley's origin. It tells the story of the primordial Buddha's enlightenment and the spread of Buddhism in Nepal.

This most sacred site has always been the most important power place for local Buddhists and for pilgrims from all over the world. It is considered to be the most powerful shrine in the Himalayas.

Indian Buddhism began to penetrate the mountain passes into Nepal in perhaps the 4th or 5th century AD, although its influence has always been mainly confined to the Kathmandu Valley as the western part of the country. With the destruction of Buddhism in India in the 13th century, Tibet, Nepal's powerful neighbour to the north, began to influence the country's religious development. However, the Tantric Buddhism that resulted became increasingly corrupt and fun with Hinduism, the predominant religion, and the two became and remain even today almost indistinguishable.

In the 1930s the first Nepalese ordained as Theravada monks in India but Nepal's Hindu ruler's refused to allow them to return to the country and imprisoned those who did With the change of government in 1950 and the coming of religious freedom, Theravada Buddhism has begun to steadily gain support. Since 1959 Tibetan refugees have also established themselves in the country and their presence has helped to some extent to revive traditional Nepalese Buddhism.

Until recently nuns in Nepal took ten precepts and did not have access to full ordination. In 1981 group of nuns went to Los Angeles, California to receive full ordination as bhikkhunis. In 1998 other Nepali nuns received bhikkhuni ordination in China and Bodhgaya, India. In 1999 in Lumb Bhikkhuni Dhammavati organised the first siksmana ordination to be held in Nepal in 1000 years.

THE HIMALAYAN KINGDOMS of Nepal and Bhutan share a history of influence by Tibet, China, and India, and an interlude of British colonial guidance. Although the kingdoms are not contiguous, each country is bordered by China to the north and India on its other peripheries. Both kingdoms are ruled by hereditary monarchs and are traditional societies with predominantly agricultural economies; their cultures, however, differ. Nepal's Hinduism, a legacy of India's influence, defines its culture and caste-structured society. Bhutan's Buddhist practices and culture reflect India's influence by way of Tibet. The two countries' legal systems also reflect their heritage. Nepal's judicial system blends Hindu legal and English common law traditions. Bhutan's legal system is based on Buddhist law and English common law.

Nepal has existed as a kingdom centered in the Kathmandu Valley for more than 1,500 years. The country is known for its majestic Himalayas and has nine of the fourteen peaks in the world over 8,000 meters, including Mount Everest and Annapurna I.

Modern Nepal began its evolution in the sixteenth century with the founding of the House of Gorkha by Dravya Shah in 1559. In the late eighteenth century, Gorkha conquests extended the kingdom through the Himalayas for almost 1,500 kilometers from the western boundary of Garhwal, India, through the territory of Sikkim in the east. In the early nineteenth century, Gorkha power came into conflict with the British East India Company. The resulting Anglo-Nepalese War (1814-16) was devastating for Nepal: the Treaty of Sagauli reduced the kingdom to the boundaries it has since occupied, less than 900 kilometers from east to west. For almost thirty years after the treaty was concluded, infighting among aristocratic factions characterized Nepal.

The next stage of Nepalese politics was the period of hereditary Rana rule—the establishment of a dictatorship of successive Rana prime ministers beginning with Jang Bahadur Kunwar in 1846.

During the period of Rana rule, which lasted until the end of 1950, Nepal was governed by a landed aristocracy; parliamentary government was in name only. This period provided stability, but also inhibited political and economic development because the Ranas isolated the country and exercised total control over internal affairs. Although during this period Nepal was a constitutional monarchy with universal suffrage granted at age eighteen, political parties were not formed until the mid-twentieth century and were later banned.

The longevity of the Rana dictatorship was also a result of a partnership between the rulers and the army. Patronage ensured loyal soldiers: the military supported the Rana prime ministers and, later, the Shah monarchs, who were figureheads during Rana rule.

In January 1951, the Ranas were forced to concede to the restoration of the monarchy, which then assumed charge of all executive powers: financial management, appointment of government officials, and command of the armed forces. The latter power became an increasingly useful tool for enforcing control. In 1962 King Mahendra Bir Bikram Shah Dev devised the centrally controlled partyless council system of government called panchayat. This system served as the institutional basis of the king's rule and was envisioned by the palace as a democratic administration although it functioned only at the king's behest. Incorporated into the 1962 constitution, the panchayat system was established at the village, district, and national levels. Successive changes in government and constitutional revisions did not weaken the powers of the absolute monarchy. In fact, a May 1980 referendum reaffirmed the status quo of the panchayat system and its continuation as a rubber stamp for the king. Elections in 1981 and 1986 were characterized by the lack of political programs.

Government by an absolute monarch behind a democratic facade lasted for some thirty years. Although many party members were exiled to India, opposition to the government and the panchayat system continued to grow, particularly in the late 1980s when the outlawed political parties announced a drive for a multiparty system. A coalition between the Nepali Congress Party and the Communist Party of Nepal was formed in late 1989. The increasing disillusionment with and unpopularity of King Birendra Bir Bikram Shah Dev's regime and the worsening economic situation caused by the trade and transit dispute with India added to the momentum of the incipient pro-democracy movement.

The dissolution of the Berlin Wall and the Soviet Union, and the successes of the pro-democracy movements in Eastern Europe in the late 1980s and early 1990s, had an impact in Nepal. In part as a result of the participatory experiences of Nepalese in India, movements arose to effect changes in Nepal's government and society. Nepal's longstanding history of continuity of rule and relative stability was challenged when the Movement for the Restoration of Democracy, or pro-democracy movement, was formally established on February 18, 1990, almost forty years after the end of Rana control. Demonstrations and rallies—accompanied by violence, arrests, and even deaths—were held throughout the country. Political unrest became widespread. Ethnic groups agitated for official recognition of their cultural heritage and linguistic tradition and demonstrated against the monarchy. The goal of the pro-democracy movement, however, was to establish a more representative democracy and to end the panchayat system.

The demonstrations and protests characterizing the pro-democracy movement gained momentum when the ban on political parties and activities was lifted in April 1990. That same month, the prime minister resigned, the Council of Ministers and the Rashtriya Panchayat (National Panchayat, or Parliament) were dissolved, and talks with the opposition were begun. A multiparty interim government replaced the panchayat system. The king nominated a four-member council, established a Constitution Recommendation Commission, and announced that he would begin an official inquiry into the deaths that had resulted from the pro-democracy demonstrations. In mid-May, a general amnesty was declared for all political prisoners. A draft constitution was announced in the summer of 1990. King Birendra wanted the draft amended to give him more leverage, but subsequent negotiations did not yield as much as he desired. In November 1990, the king finally approved and promulgated a new, more democratic constitution that vested sovereignty in the people.

The panchayat system finally ended in May 1991, when general elections, deemed "generally fair, free, and open" by an international election inspection team, were held. Approximately 65 percent of the populace voted. Although more than forty political parties registered with the election commission, only twenty political parties—mostly small, communist splinter groups—were on the ballot. The Nepali Congress Party won 110 of the 205 seats in the House of Representatives, and the Communist Party of Nepal (United Marxist-Leninist) won 69 seats. Previously operating in exile and behind the scenes, the various communist and other parties and coalitions became a powerful presence in the newly constituted bicameral Parliament. Nepal continued its gradual move toward a multiparty democracy.

Pro-democracy protests continued unabated. Demonstrations were held on February 18,1992, the second anniversary of the founding of the pro-democracy movement. In early April 1992, rival student groups clashed, and communist and leftist opposition groups called for a general strike as a response to double digit inflation and a more than 60 percent increase in water and electricity tariffs. As a result of skirmishes between the police and demonstrators, a curfew was imposed. In addition, the government banned primary and secondary schoolteachers from political activities and from joining or campaigning for political parties.

Elections to the village development committees and municipalities were held in late May 1992; the elections pitted the various communist factions and other parties against the Nepali Congress Party administration of Prime Minister Girija Prasad (G.P.) Koirala. More than 90,000 civilian and security personnel were assigned to safeguard the elections. In contrast to the May 1991 parliamentary election, the Nepali Congress Party routed the communists in the urban areas and even made some gains in the rural areas. The Nepali Congress Party won 331 positions, or 56 percent of the seats, in the municipalities; the Communist Party of Nepal (United Marxist-Leninist) won 119 seats, or 20 percent of the seats; and other lesser parties won the remainder of the seats. In newly established village development committees, the Nepali Congress Party won 21,461 positions; the Communist Party of Nepal (United Marxist-Leninist) won 11,175 seats.

The Nepalese army has long been intertwined with the monarchy; the 1990 constitution, however, changed the relationship between the military and the king. For the first time, the military no longer was solely an instrument of the king; it was also subordinate to the authority of Parliament. Although under the constitution the king retains his title as the supreme commander of the army the functional commander in chief is appointed on the recommendation of the prime minister. Although both the king and the government are responsible for implementing national security and military policy, the king's power to declare a state of national emergency and to conduct foreign affairs has national security implications.

Nepal is noted for its famed Gurkha soldiers. Gurkhas served both at home and abroad in the British, Indian, Singapore, and Brunei armies. Their remittances to Nepal were of primary importance to the economy and served as an important source of foreign exchange. By 1997, however, the number of Gurkhas serving in the British army is expected to be reduced from 8,000 to 2,500 persons, and the Gurkha garrison in Hong Kong is scheduled to be withdrawn gradually in the period up to 1995. As of April 1992, a token number of Gurkhas was serving in a United Nations peacekeeping force in the former Yugoslavia.

The difficulty of replacing Nepal's long tradition of autocracy with a democracy, coupled with the economic challenges posed by physical geography and location, was daunting. As of 1992, many of the prescribed changes had only just been instituted, or were still to come. Many observers expected that the populist experiment of a multiparty democracy would meet with eventual failure and that the monarchy and the army would return to some type of power-sharing formula.

Nepal's population, estimated in 1990 as approximately 19.1 million, is very diverse. The country is home to more than a dozen ethnic groups, which originate from three major ethnic divisions: Indo-Nepalese, Tibeto-Nepalese, and indigenous Nepalese. Ethnic identity—distinguished primarily by language and dress—constrains the selection of a spouse, friendships, and career, and is evident in social organization, occupation, and religious observances. Hinduism is the official religion of Nepal, although, in fact, the religion practiced by the majority of Nepalese is a synthesis of Hinduism and Buddhism and the practices have intermingled over time. The socio-economic ramifications of the country's diversity have proven problematic for Nepal in the late twentieth century.

Considered a least-developed country, Nepal depends heavily on farming, which accounts for most of the country's gross domestic product. The work force is largely unskilled and mostly illiterate. Nepal's industrial base was established in the 1930s, but little process has been made in improving economic performance. In the early 1990s, tourism was one of the largest sources of foreign exchange; visitors from the United States were the most numerous.

Social status in Nepal is measured by economic standing Landownership is both a measure of status and a source of income. Women occupy a secondary position, particularly in business and the civil service, although the constitution guarantees equality between men and women. Nepalese tribal and communal customs dictate women's lesser role in society, but their status differs from one ethnic group to another and is usually determined by caste.

As of 1992, education was free and compulsory for five years; however males had literacy rates about three times higher than the rates for females and higher school enrollment levels. There were relatively few other social services in the country. The absence of modern medical care, clean drinking water, and adequate sanitation resulted in the prevalence of gastrointestinal diseases. Malnutrition was also a problem, particularly in rural areas. A period of drought in 1992 was expected to cause further food shortages, especially of grain. The country has consistently had high morbi. ity and death rates.

Economic assistance from other countries, especially India, has been vital to Nepal. Since the 1980s, however, bilateral aid and multilateral assistance programs from countries other than India have been an increasingly important part of development planning. Nepal has received aid from both the United States and communist countries.

In the late twentieth century, Nepal's foreign policy continued to be affected by its geostrategic location between China and India and its attempt to maintain a balance between these powerful neighbors. Nepal's relationship with India is governed by the 1950 Treaty of Peace and Friendship and its accompanying letters, which established an informal military alliance whereby both countries are required to consult and "devise effective countermeasures" in case the security of either is threatened. Since the 1970s, however, Nepal has exhibited greater independence in its foreign policy, establishing bilateral diplomatic relations with other countries and joining various multilateral and regional organizations.

Nepal, for example, belongs to the United Nations and its affiliated agencies such as the Group of 77, as well as the Nonaligned Movement and the Asian Development Bank. It is also a member of the South Asian Association for Regional Cooperation (SAARC), founded in 1983, initially under a slightly different name, as an institutionalized framework for regional cooperation; its permanent secretariat was established in 1987 in Kathmandu. It does not accept compulsory United Nations International Court of Justice jurisdiction.

One of India's longstanding sources of power over Nepal has been India's control of access to raw materials and supply routes. The effect of this control was especially evident during the 1989 trade and transit dispute—and its aftermath—when the foreign trade balance was negatively affected and the economy took a downturn.

In early 1992, Nepal's relations with India were clouded by controversy over the December 1991 agreement for cooperation on a hydroelectric and irrigation project at Tanakpur, near the southwestern Nepalese—Indian border. The Communist Party of Nepal (United Marxist-Leninist) and other leftist parties opposed the project, which they regarded as against Nepal's national interest because the site, on Nepalese territory, was not covered by a formal treaty. The constitution stipulates that treaties need parliamentary assent if exploitation of the nation's natural resources is involved. Prime Minister G.P. Koirala said he had signed a memorandum of understanding, not a treaty. The opposition took their case to the Supreme Court.

Military relations between Kathmandu and New Delhi were cordial. In March 1992, the Indian chief of army staff visited Nepal and was made an honorary general of the Royal Nepal Army, an uncommon occurrence.

Nepal's relations with China were low-key and an exercise in caution. Nonetheless, India interpreted sales of air defense weapons by China to Nepal in 1988 as interfering with its treaty arrangements with Nepal. Nepal and China, however, signed technical and economic cooperation agreements in March 1992.

Bhutan has its own distinct history, although it shares Nepal's Himalayan geography and neighbors. Only one-third the size of Nepal, Bhutan also has a much smaller population: estimated at about 600,000 persons in 1990 as compared to a population of over 19 million in Nepal.

The precursor of Bhutan, the state of Lhomon or Monyul, was said to have existed between 500 B.C. and 600 A.D. At the end of that period, Buddhism was introduced into the country; a branch of Mahayana Buddhism is the state religion of Bhutan. Bhutan was subject to both Indian and Tibetan influences, and small independent monarchies began to develop in the country by the early ninth century. Religious rivalry among various Buddhist subsects also influenced political development; the rivalry began in the tenth century and continued through the seventeenth century, when a theocratic government independent of Tibetan political influence united the country. From that time until 1907, the Kingdom of Bhutan, or Drukyul (literally land of the Thunder Dragon), had a dual system of shared civil and spiritual (Buddhist) rule. In 1907 the absolute monarchy was established, and the hereditary position of Druk Gyalpo, or Dragon King, was awarded to the powerful Wangchuck family. Since 1972, Jigme Singye Wangchuck has held the position of Druk Gyalpo.

The Druk Gyalpo controls the executive, legislative, and judicial branches of the government. The monarchy is absolute, but the king is admired and respected and is referred to by the people as "our King." The Council of Ministers and Royal Advisory Council are part of the executive branch of government. The legislative branch is made up of the unicameral National Assembly, or Tshogdu whose members are either indirectly elected or appointed by the Druk Gyalpo. Bhutan has neither a written constitution nor organic laws. The 1953 royal decree on the Constitution of the National Assembly is the primary legal, or constitutional, basis for that body and sets forth its rules and procedures. The Supreme Court of Appeal, in effect the Druk Gyalpo, is the highest-level court; judges are appointed by the Druk Gyalpo. There are no lawyers. The civil code and criminal code are based on seventeenth-century concepts.

Under Jigme Singye Wangchuck, Bhutan's centrally controlled government system has been instrumental in initiating greater political participation. In the early 1990s, however, there were still no legal political parties—although there were elite political factions—and no national elections. There was no overt communist presence. Each family was allowed one vote in village-level elections. Local government was divided into zones, districts, sub-districts, and village groups, and meetings were regularly held at the village and block (gewog) levels, where issues were decided by public debate. The complex administrative network of consultation and decision-making by consensus obscured the need for national elections. At the 1992 session of the National Assembly, support for the hereditary monarchy was unanimously reaffirmed.

Like Nepal, Bhutan has a diverse population. It is home to four ethnic groups: Ngalop—of Tibetan origin; Sharchop-of Indo-Mongoloid origin; aboriginal, or indigenous, tribal peoples; and Nepalese. In the early 1990s, the first three groups made up about 72 percent of the population. According to this estimate, the Nepalese comprised approximately 28 percent of the population; other estimates suggested that 30 to 40 percent might be Nepalese. The Nepalese constituted a majority in southern Bhutan, where, in an effort to maintain traditional culture and control, the government has tried to confine their immigration and restrict their residence and employment. In the early 1990s, only approximately 15 percent of the Nepalese in Bhutan were considered legal permanent residents; only those immigrants who had resided in Bhutan for fifteen or twenty years—the number of years depended on their occupational status and other criteria—were considered for citizenship. Nepalese immigrants who were asked to leave because their claims to citizenship did not conform to the 1985 Citizenship Act openly voiced their discontent with the government. Illegal immigrants often were militant anti-nationals.

In the 1980s, the Bhutanese, believing their identity threatened by absorption of a growing Nepalese minority and the specter of annexation by India, promulgated a policy of *driglam namzha*, "national customs and etiquette." This policy, sought to preserve and enhance Bhutanese cultural identity and bolster Bhutanese nationalism. The policy mandated the wearing of national dress for formal occasions and the use of the official language, Dzongkha, in schools. In 1989, it was decreed that Nepali, which had been offered as an optional language, was no longer to be taught in the schools.

Subsequent government decrees contributed to a growing conflict with ethnic Nepalese, who sought to maintain their own identity and viewed these edicts as restrictive. Ethnic strife increased as the aftereffects of Nepal's pro-democracy movement spread to Bhutan, where Nepalese communities demonstrated against the government in an effort to protect their rights from the *driglam namzha* policy. Expatriate Nepalese political groups in Nepal and India supported these anti-government activities, further alienating the Bhutanese.

Bhutan's military force, the Royal Bhutan Army, is very small; in 1990 it numbered only 6,000 persons. The Druk Gyalpo is the supreme commander of the army, but daily operations are the responsibility of the chief operations officer. The army's primary mission is border defense although it also assists the Royal Bhutan Police in internal security matters.

Bhutan, like Nepal, is considered a least-developed country. Its work force is largely unskilled, and a wide gap exists between the rich and the poor. Farming is the mainstay of the economy and accounts for most of the gross domestic product. Although Bhutan did not begin to establish its industrial base until the 1950s, careful economic planning and use of foreign aid have resulted in measurable improvements in economic efficiency and performance over the last four decades. As is the case in Nepal, tourists bring in a major portion of the country's foreign exchange.

Social status in Bhutan, as in Nepal, depends primarily on economic standing in the community. Specifically, it depends on landownership, occupation, and perceived religious authority. The society is male dominated. Although as of 1992 the government officially encouraged increased participation of women in political and administrative life, women remained in a secondary position, particularly in business and the civil service. Bhutanese women, however, do have a dominant social position, and land often passes to daughters, not to sons. Bhutan's traditional society is both matriarchal and patriarchal; the head of the family is the member in highest esteem. However, men predominate in government and have more opportunities for higher education than do women.

As of 1992, education in Bhutan is free for eleven years but not compulsory. Men have literacy rates about three times higher than those for women, and school enrollment levels are higher for males.

As is the case in Nepal, social services are not widespread. Modern medical care is lacking, as is clean drinking water and adequate sanitation. Not surprisingly, gastrointestinal diseases are widespread. Nutrional deficiencies are also prevalent; serious malnutrition, however, does not appear to be a problem. Like Nepal, the country had high morbidity and death rates in the early 1990s.

Foreign aid, grants, and concessionary loans constituted a large percentage of Bhutan's budget in the early 1990s. Like Nepal, Bhutan received foreign assistance from the United Nations, the Colombo Plan, the Asian Development Bank, the World Bank, and the Organization of Petroleum Exporting Countries, as well as official development assistance and other official flows. Because Bhutan had no formal diplomatic relations with the United States as of 1992, no official aid was forthcoming from Washington.

As has been the case in Nepal, Bhutan's foreign policy has been affected by its geo-strategic location. From the seventh century until 1860, the country's foreign policy was influenced by Tibet; next followed a period of British guidance over foreign affairs. After India received independence from Britain in 1947, Bhutan came under India's influence. Thimphu and New Delhi's relationship is governed by the 1949 Treaty of Friendship between the Government of India and the Government of Bhutan—in force in perpetuity—which calls for peace and noninterference in internal affairs and New Delhi's guidance and advice in external relations. Like Nepal, however, Bhutan is exhibiting greater independence in its foreign policy, and by the early 1990's was, in effect, autonomous in its foreign relations. Thimphu has established bilateral diplomatic relations with other countries and has joined various multilateral and regional organizations. Bhutan belongs to the United Nations, as well as to organizations such as SAARC, the Nonaligned Movement, and the Asian Development Bank. It does not accept compulsory United Nations International Court of Justice jurisdiction.

Both Nepal and Bhutan were facing refugee problems in the early 1 990s; statistics on the number of refugees come from diverse sources and are discrepant. In April 1992, the United Nations High Commissioner for Refugees estimated that since 1986 more than 30,000 ethnic Nepalese had left Bhutan because of political discontent, poor employment prospects, or because they were considered illegal immigrants. A much higher figure is projected by G.P. Koirala, Nepal's prime minister, who has estimated that in the early 1990s Nepalese from Bhutan seeking to escape the sanctions imposed by *driglam namzha* arrived in Nepal at the rate of 200 persons daily.

Anti-nationals in Bhutan used the growing number of southern Bhutanese-Nepalese in the refugee camps within Nepal as a means to publicize and internationalize their plight. To this end, they encouraged Nepalese to leave Bhutan and also encouraged Nepalese from India to enter the camps. For Bhutan, the departure of the Nepalese often meant the loss of skilled laborers however it also resulted in the exodus of unwanted agitators. For Nepal, the refugees were an added economic burden—more people needing housing, food, clothing, education, and other social services. Living conditions in the refugee camps within Nepal were reported to be poor. As of mid-1992, the camps were filled with people holding Nepalese citizenship cards, Bhutanese citizenship cards, and UNHCR certificates attesting they were "Bhutanese refugees". However, because each party seeks to present its own case, all statistics and statements related to the Nepalese refugee situation must be viewed cautiously.

The refugee problem presented a challenge to India, which needed to balance its interests in maintaining Bhutan's stability with the necessity of not inflaming nationalist passions among its own ethnic Nepalese population and not upsetting its relations with either Nepal or Bhutan. India would not allow its territory to be used as a staging ground for protests by Bhutanese residents of Nepalese origin. The situation was further complicated by the fact that Indian laborers who entered Nepal in search of work displaced underemployed and unemployed Nepalese workers.

September 10,1992

Since the introduction was written, the events of late 1992 and early 1993 in Nepal and Bhutan have been a continuum of the past few years. The refugee issue has continued to be problematic. The leaders of both Nepal and Bhutan met with India's leaders in late 1992 and early 1993; all the parties reaffirmed that the issue was an internal matter that should be resolved through bilateral talks between Nepal and Bhutan. In spite of the agitation and activities of anti-nationals in the south, Bhutan's National Assembly passed a National Security Act in late 1992 that abolished the death penalty for crimes of treason as stipulated in a 1957 law, providing instead for life imprisonment.

In December 1992, the Supreme Court of Nepal ruled against Prime Minister G.P. Koirala's signing of a December 1991 accord for hydroelectric power cooperation with India at Tanakpur. After their victory, Koirala's opponents in the Nepal Communist Party (United Marxist-Leninist) pressed him to step down—he refused. As a result of the court's decision, however, Kathmandu said the Koirala government would present the Tanakpur accord and its relevant documents to the next parliamentary session for ratification—a step that would have otherwise been bypassed.

Nepal also passed laws in December 1992 to encourage foreign (and local) investment by creating a more favorable investment environment. Foreigners will be allowed to repatriate earnings and hold total equity in new projects.

Nepal: A Cultural Perspective

Hinduism and Buddhism are the two prominent religions in Nepal, the key features of these religious are presented in this book. Nepal is unique in the world in that an ideal harmony can be seen between Hinduism and Buddhism. This harmony is manifested by the mutual respect and religious practice followed by the Hindus and the Buddhists. These religions attach higher values to morality rather than the material growth and commercialization. so an explanation of the present state of development of Nepal may be inherent here.

Festivals and rituals help promote group cohesion and solidarity. Their practice perpetuates one's traditions and maintains cultural heritage. An attempt has been made to describe some of the main festivals of Nepal and life cycle rituals to offer a bird's-eye view of Nepal's culture.

The second part in devoted to the land, people and economy. We believe that all socio-economic and cultural weaknesses and/or constraints can be converted into opportunities of proper strategies are developed. But Nepal's geo-political situation until now has been more an obstacle to change and development than a strength. There is a pervasive mindset in Nepal that it is a small country and that unless it is aided and abetted by India and China, it is destined to perish. So most of Nepal's development practice is governed by this feeling of interiority and full to partial surrender. The donors, too, are convinced of this and have exerted enough pressure on Nepal to make its policies relevant to these neighbors, particularly India.

Nepal is a plural society with a plethora of rich cultural diversity. Within an area of 55,000 square miles, this rectangular shaped country has spectacular ecological variations. It is a multi-cultural.,multi-lingual and multi-religious country. It has flat plain land most suitable to agriculture and mid-hills with tremendous potentials for horticultural enterprises, forests and water resources. The majestic mountains are unmatched anywhere in the world. They attract hundreds of thousands of tourists and mountaineers. Much of the potential still remains to be exploited.

The economy has not gained any momentum because the rate of population growth almost equals the poor rate of agricultural growth. There has been similarly poor performance in the areas of trade industry and public finance.

Within this context, we have identified the socio-economic, political, environment and women's and gender-related issues as the important ones that merit immediate attention. These contemporary issues are described in part three of this book.

Unplanned migration (hill to Tarai rural-urban and international) has created significant social problems, such as environmental degradation, pressure on social services and loss of job opportunities. The adoption of liberal economic policies without adequate preparation has hindered native industries which are still at the embryonic stages. Half of the population is under the poverty line. Women are one of the most disadvantaged segments of the population. They are not in the mainstream of development. Their life expectancy is less than that of the male population. The average life expectancy of the Nepalese is also one of the lowest in the world. Unchecked population growth has a tremendous negative impact on forest resources and the environment. Landslides, forest degradation, and water and air pollution are problems. Political stability was assumed to be a precondition to economic progress, but three decades of the Panchayat system did not result in any economic progress. The progress made after the introduction of the parliamentary multiparty democratic system in 1990 is also not noteworthy. There has been a gradual erosion of ethics and morality among the majority of the politicians in the country, and people at large have lost their faith in the politicians. This chapter concludes with a section on ethnicity and nation building. It has been argued that ethnic and caste groups are mutually inclusive constructs, not mutually exclusive constructs. It is debated that the conventional ethnic-caste paradigm of understanding the Nepal society is a faulty and unscientific approach.

Most of the people in Nepal are engaged in agriculture. This sector has been a major area of focus in most of the country's five-year plans. However, the conditions of the majority of the farmers have not improved nor has this sector significantly helped in improving the economy of the country as a whole. Nepal was an exporter of food grains until recently but after the mid-1980s, it became a food-importing nation. Farming is subsistence in nature, and the yields of important food crops have either remained constant or declined. The land distribution is skewed, and the average size of land holdings is very small—less than a hectare for an average family size of six.

Community forestry has had some positive impact on the management of forests, and it has been found that the more the beneficiary farmers participate in forest management, the better the forest is managed. But the handing over of the national forests to the forests user groups has been a slow process.

The national parks have been able to conserve biodiversity, but a much needs to be done to secure the participation of the people surrounding the national parks.

The status of forests in terms of the crown percentage has declined. The Nepali government is hesitant to commercialize the forest resources. It is fair to say that the government is probably losing more by not scientifically harvesting and managing the forest resource than by preserving most of the over-matured forest resources, including the hardwood timber.

Water resources have not been harnessed properly. Progress irrigation development has been very slow — most of the farming in Nepal is still dependent on monsoon rain. Though farmer-managed irrigation systems have been found to be more effective and efficient, the government has yet been unable to modify its larger-scale irrigation efforts to achieve similar effectiveness. Unfortunately small-scale farmer-managed irrigation schemes cannot really fulfill the vast need for irrigation water.

The poor situation in the natural resources arena has had a tremendous, deleterious impact on the majority of the people. They are mostly poor and illiterate, and health care is not within the reach of the majority of the population.

Political change was thought to be the panacea for all sorts of human misery in Nepal, because the multiparty parliamentary democratic system would empower the Nepalese people. But, in spite of the political change a decade ago, and ultimately to their great despair, the majority of the people have remained untouched; they are still not partners in development. People's aspirations have not been realized and the pace of development has been very slow. Corruption and greed tend to be globalized and Nepal has been a fertile land for their nurturing. The externalities have been instrumental in helping a new rich class evolve that is loyal to foreign concepts and ideas and are readily prepared to experiment in Nepali soil without bothering to test first and modify. It is this group of people who are politically and economically dominant in Nepal while the majority of the Nepalese have been left behind. If this trend continues, people could unite and revolt against what is happening for greater justice and peace.

2

Nepal: Society and Culture

"Caste" defines certain groups in a hierarchy of ritual purity and pollution and prescribes inter-group behavior in certain spheres, particularly marriage and commensality (Bennett, 1983). Kroeber defined caste as an endogamous and hereditary subdivision of an ethnic unit occupying a positron of superior or inferior rank or social esteem in comparison with other such divisions (Kroeber, 1930). This definition assumes caste systems as system of social stratification- i.e., an aggregate of ranked people that is unusually rigid and birth ascribed and permits no individual mobility. A Caste system can be said to occur, says Berreman (1965) when a society is composed of birth-ascribed, hierarchically ordered and culturally distinct groups (castes).

Social stratification occurs in every society. Citing from Sorokin, Klauss (1980) mentions that social stratification means differentiation of a given population into hierarchically superposed classes. It is manifested in the existence of upper and lower layers. Its basis and very essence consist in an unequal distribution of rights and privileges, duties and responsibilities, social values and privations, social power and influences among the members of a society. Stratification is a system by which adult members of a society enjoy differential rights of access to basic resources. These resources may be the physical things needed to sustain life, either directly (air, water and food) or indirectly (things that can not themselves be consumed but are required to obtain other things) outstanding examples of the latter are land raw materials for tools, water for irrigation and materials to build a shelter. The presence or absence of differential access to basic resources can be obvious from the fact that either such resources are free to all or certain persons or groups have control of them and all others must apply to the controllers for access.

Membership in castes is determined by birth. A common means of guaranteeing this status is by prescribing endogamous marriage in the caste and ascribing to the child the caste affiliation of its parents. That a caste system is a hierarchy implies that it is a system of differential evaluation-differential power and rewards, and differential association; in short a system of institutionalized inequality Castes are ranked ultimately in terms of the shared "intrinsic worth" that is ascribed by birth to the individuals who constitute them. This criterion of rank may be defined and expressed in many idioms such as purity (as in India), honor (as in Swat) or genetically determined capabilities (as in the United States), but always those who are high regard themselves as more worthy than those who are low (Berreman, 1965).

We view a caste system as different from a class system. Unlike the caste system, a class system defines the rank of its members according to their individual attributes and behavior. A member in a particular caste exhibits attributes of that particular caste because he is a member of it. In a class system, one is a member of a class because he displays the attributes of that class. Individual mobility is theoretically impossible in a rigid caste system, but it is not so in a class system.

Nepal is well known to the world for its majestic mountains and heroic people, the Gorkhas It has nurtured two great religions of the world, Hinduism and Buddhism, and maintained the religious and ethnic/caste coexistence. It is in Nepal that the Hindu and Buddhist civilizations dovetail and merge. Nepal is an ancient civilization; so are its society and culture. Though religion has always been a central feature of Nepali life, in fact we have never encountered any religions fanaticism in Nepal (Bista, 1994). On the contrary, Nepalese celebrate colorful festivals, observe various rituals, and respect and accommodate diverse religious traditions. Prominent are Shamanism, Shaivism, Buddhism, Trantrism and Vaishnavism.

In the past Nepal's socio economic situation and, more so, the South Asian socio economic situation were characterized by the absence of stratification and the presence of equalitarian social groups that became transformed, over time, into a complex stratified caste system (Klass, 1980).

In ancient Nepal, the society was equalitarian. The caste concept was introduced in Nepal in the beginning of the Lichhavi era in the form of Vaishnavism, and when it did arrive it had to adapt itself not only to Shamanism and Shaivism but also to Buddhism (Bista, 1994). The Nepal people appear to have preferred an open social order rather than one based on caste principal's as is prevalent in India, where there is much emphasis on the dialectics of the pure and impure (Dumont, 1970).

Hindu caste culture has a varied presence in Nepal, in terms of its prevalence and its significance.

It was during the 4th century that king Jayasthiti Malla introduced caste principles and conduct in Kathmandu valley (Bista, 1994). But native people in the Kathmandu valley continued their own ways of religious practices, unlike the Hindu code of conduct. Kathmandu valley was effectively closed toward the latter part of Malla period. During the 15th century, in king Pratap Malla's period the people of Kathmandu valley came to be known as Newars and the land as Nepal (Acharyn, 1952; Doherty, 1978; Malla, 1981; Bista, 1994). During the 18th century, when the country expanded and several smaller states were merged into Nepal, the Newar people were treated as a separate ethnic group. Jang Bahadur, the first Rana prime minister in the 19th century, to raise his own status succeeded in introducing caste system to a much greater degree than the Malla king who did this 400 years before him. All Newari-speaking people were put into a single caste category at the lower level, known in local parlance as Matwali, meaning liquor drinkers. But during that time, among the Newars a complex caste system developed. The classical Varna model, as prescribed in the ancient codes as the Manusmritri (Brahmin > Khatriya > Vaishya > Shudra (Touchable and Untouchable) does not exist in Nepal and has been modified to suit the local situation. Neverthless, discrimination based on caste was legally abolished in 1963.

Ram Shah (1606-33), the king of the ancient kingdom of Gorkha, Nepal introduced a comprehensive legal code for the first time outside the Kathmandu valley in the Gandaki region. Prescriptions of regulation of behavior according to caste hierarchy were largely ignored. King Prithvinarayan Shah, the descendent of Ram Shah, considered Nepal a garden of four castes and 36 ethnic groups, which he called *"Chhattis Varna"*. Stiller (1968) maintains that Prithvinarayan Shah had soldiers from four different peoples—Magars, Brahmins, Thakuri and Khas. Ram Shah's code appealed to all Nepalese, who responded to its innate egalitarianism, a sense of justice for all, unlike the Manusmriti codes, which promised legal discrimination and institutionalized social oppression.

People along the mid hills of Nepal were gradually influenced by the Brahmanic culture and to achieve social status, most of the Khas people coveted the title of Thakuri Chhetri (Matwali Chhetri or simply Matawali) (Sharma, 1971).

Dor B Bista (1994) maintains that Bahun rituals involved frequent bathing in fresh water. It became difficult to adhere to such practice in the high mountain regions with cold water. The northern Himalayan region was inhabited by the people of Tibetan origin who followed Tibetan form of Buddhism -Lamaism.

In Tarai, the southern belt of Nepal, three distinct cultural groups practice three different religions. In the eastern Tarai, among most of the Maithili-speaking people the caste system is intact. In the western Tarai, Tharus are the native people, and they practice Shamanistic religious practices The third group who moved into the parts of Tarai (east and west) is the Mohammedan people who adhere to Islam.

Most of the Kirat people in the astern hills practiced the Kirat religion with its gods and goddesses, priests and spirit mediums. The Hindu caste system was less successful in the east than the west. Caplan (1970) maintained that the real practitioners of Hinduism were taken by the Kiratis as attempted political and cultural intrusion by the Kathmandu authorities and were resisted as a politically subversive force. Those high caste Hindus who entered the eastern mountains and hills rather considerably modified their own lifestyle.

The Nepal version of a caste system is not simple. It encompasses not only the Nepali-speaking hill people or the hill Hindu castes but also the numerous Newari-speaking castes of all ranks, the many Tibeto-Burman ethnic groups, the Tibetan-speaking Bhote groups from the high mountain regions, and the Muslim Hindu and indigenous populations of the southern Tarai belt (Hofer, 1979).

The caste system in Nepal is of recent origin. Within a few centuries of its introduction, there was a realization that it was doing more harm than good and so it was abolished. Strict adherence to the brutal code of conduct in any real sense was never observed among the greater segment of the Hindu population in Nepal. Nepal's pluralism and diversity were recognized and respected by the rulers of the country. Social interaction between the caste and non-caste groups of the Nepali population has shaped the Nepal Society as a mosaic of diverse cultures where caste and non-caste groups have partially or fully internalized one another's ways of living

Unlike in any fanatic society, in Nepal there has been a vertical mobility among castes and there is no sanction to it. This has been generally possible due to education, migration and inter-caste marriage practices More recently, we have observed that people who make good business are economically better off, and the economic factor has much stronger influence on social status with a bearing in upward caste mobility. As the caste system is getting weaker and weaker, the trend towards a less discriminatory society is obvious.

No one should be misled, however, that caste has no bearing at all in influencing sociopolitical and economic decisions. In caste societies, the dominant caste(s) have exercised the power in an attempt to maintain the *status quo*, just as the dominant group in a plural society.

Caste and ethnic affiliation have influenced the division of the people during election times in Nepal. During social conflict, people have partitioned along caste/ethnic lines. There has always been tension and conflict of various degrees, which become not only obvious, but at times subversive After each conflict, the caste/ethnic power balance changes and in some cases, an improvement in caste/ethnic relations occurs.

Religion

Religion in contemporary Western thought has been increasingly considered a matter of belief and individual intellectual commitment, specifically opposed to ritual conformity, which is often considered empty of meaning and not compatible with the full development of the personality" (Douglas, 1970), Religion is understood in two ways. The substantive definition entails religion as a system of communally experienced beliefs and practices (institutions) oriented toward a culturally defined supernatural, transcendent realm/beings. It defines what religion is. The functional definition (defines what religion does for individuals and social groups) assumes religion as a system of symbols that acts to establish powerful, pervasive and long-lasting moods and motivations in people by formulating conceptions of a general order of existence and clothing these conceptions with such an aura of factuality that moods and motivations sect uniquely realistic.

Within Nepal religion, which in the Nepal language is known as *Dharma,* has a broader meaning. It also means duty, ethics morality, rule, merit and pious acts. In Nepal's context, people speak of *Dharma* as something one does (or at least should do), rather than something one believes in. In Nepali usage, *Dharma* encompasses the performance of specified rites and ceremonies and obedience to ritual prescriptions appropriate to one's place in the social structure as well as general ethical behavior covering individual actions of compassion, honesty, etc. (Bennett 1983). Religion has always been a central feature of Nepali life, and Nepal has been a meeting ground for diverse religions. Religious fanaticism is unknown in Nepal. On the contrary, the Nepalese have traditionally observed colorful rituals of various caste and ethnic groups. Though Nepal is constitutionally a Hindu kingdom, the Nepalese adhere to various religions. Hinduism and Buddhism are the two major religions practiced by the majority of the Nepalese.

Hinduism

Hinduism is believed to have started with Sruti, which literally means, "which is heard". The great philosophers, called Rishis, perfected themselves by meditation and are said to have heard in their hearts Eternal Truths, taught to their disciples telepathically. Vedas and Upanishads were in Sruti form for a long time. The original name of Hinduism was Sanatana-Dharma, meaning "righteousness forever". The word "Hind" originated from the root word "Indus". Some say, the word originated from a Persian word meaning "river people". Hindu scriptures are written in the Sanskrit language.

The term "Hinduism" has been derived from "Hindu". The non-Muslim people of the south Asian subcontinent called Hindu had no precise world for religions. They were into hundreds on communities and ethnic groups, each having its own religious beliefs, rituals, modes of worship, etc. Finding it difficult to get the names of the religions of these communities, British writers gave them the word "Hinduism" to be used as a common name for all the religions in about 1830. No one actually could be credited to the founder of Hinduism. Some historians trace the beginning of Hinduism to the third millennium B.C. long before Jesus Christ, nomadic tribes came to India and settled on the banks of the rivers Indus, Ganga and Brahmaputra. The tribes were called the Aryans Alter their settlement a Thinking process started that became known as Hinduism.

Hinduism is the religion of the Hindus, a name given to the universal religion that hailed supreme in India It is the oldest of all living religions. It is not grounded by any prophet. Hinduism is also known by the names of *Sanatana-Dharm* and *Vaidik-Dharma*.

Sanatana-Dharma means "eternal religion". Hinduism is as old as the world itself. Hinduism is the mother of all religions. Hindu scriptures are the oldest in the world. *Sanatana-Dharma* is so called, not only because it can eternal, but also because it is protected by God and because it cal make us eternal. *Vaidika-Dharma* means "the religion of the Vedas". The Vedas are the foundational scriptures of Hinduism. Hinduism is the dominant religion of the vast Indian subcontinent, and since the beginning of its history, it has profoundly influenced the lives and thoughts of countless millions. It has left an indelible impression on the entire culture of Hindus, on philosophy, art, architecture, politics, social activities. It is believed that religion gives to a Hindu equanimity of mind in prosperity and adversity, courage to face the problems of his life and a vision of his ultimate spiritual destiny.

Hinduism is not a set of abstract theories unrelated to life or a pile of religious dogmas to be accepted with blind faith, and it promises to its devotees a direct insight into reality and the grounds for the acceptance of that insight. Philosophy saved the Hindu from religious intolerance, and religion save him from the ivory-tower attitude of cold intellectualism.

In the Hindu tradition, religion saves the aspiring devotee from avoidable errors and pitfalls, work purifies his heart meditation creates concentration of mind and thought process, love gives him the urge to move forward, faith supports him with courage in the hours of despair and the grace of God bestows upon him the final fruit of liberation. •

The Pantheism of Hinduism

Orthodox Hindus have believed in every kind of theism (belief in the existence of a god) polytheism (many gods) and pantheism (worship of all gods of different creeds, cults or peoples indifferently). They have worshipped any object that they preferred, or practically none. They followed any standard of moratlity or almost none, Yet they have been recognized as Hindus in good and regular standing as long as they have not flagrantly violated the rules of caste or for that offence been out-cast

It is be noted slid Hindus worship goddesses, too. Saraswati is the Goddess of wisdom. Kali is the goddess of strength, and Laxmi is the goddess of wealth. They are worshiped by all the Hindus.

Partial Amalgamation and the Concept of Incarnation (Avatara)

With a view to unifying this mushrooming pantheon, the monotheistic philosophy that was propagated here is one God, one supreme reality (Brahman) and various personified gods, goddesses and animistic objects of worship are incarnations or gods. While God himself was indestructible, the various incarnations in which he descended to Earth in the form of an ordinary mortal had to go through the cycle of birth and death. The incarnation idea helped to partially unify the plethora of deities as different manifestations of a single divine entity. It also facilitated the absorption of deities from other religions and tribal cults, which had been outside the pale of Hinduism.

Many deities are themselves the results of amalgamation of more than two deities. For instance, we have Hari-Hara, who is an amalgamation of Hari (Krishna who is an incarnation of Vishnu) and Hara (Shiva). This amalgamation of the two recognized principal deities Vishnu and Shiva was undertaken to ease out the dualism in the Hindu religion due to the existence or the two principal sects, Vaishnavism (worshippers of Vishnu) and

Shaivism (worshippers of Shiva), who were frequently at loggerheads with each other.

Hindu Artifacts

One can't find a Hindu temple without an idol. Any object to be worshipped has to be personified. Propitiation of the gods takes place through the chanting of hymns (mantras) by a priest. But as mentioned elsewhere, the blending of different religions over generations has given rise to significant exchange of customs traditions, beliefs, rituals, etc., among the various religions. Purification is highly valued, and it is usually done after sprinkling holy water with bands and legs properly washed and prayers properly performed. River bathing in the morning among the Hindus is an auspicious act. Fire plays a pivotal role in consecrating religious ceremonies, marriages, etc. The vermilion (red powder) and saffron / white Tika, in the case of a widow, on the forehead and along with the tuft of hair as the pigtail (Tupi) and the sacred thread (Janai) are the external symbols that proclaims person's adherence to high class Hinduism. Saffron is thought to be an auspicious color. Ascetics (Sadhus and Sanyasis) also wear clothes of this color. A flag is placed on the top of a temple. Hindus greet each other with two hands (palms) joined together and by saying "Namaskar".

The Key Features of Hinduism

The Four Ashrams (stages of life): Traditionally the life of a person (100 years) was divided into four stages-. Brahmacharya (childhood and celibate youth), Grihasthram (householder), Vanaprastha (devotion to spiritual pursuit) and Sanyas (ascetic).

The first 25 years for a Hindu youth was for acquiring education, during which he would observe sexual abstinence. After this stage, he would marry and become a householder and discharge his familial and social obligation. By 50, he gradually detaches himself from worldly activities and engages in meditation. At 75, he would renounce the world and become a recluse and concentrate upon the spiritual quest. The external signs of a person becoming a Sanyasi were the unshorn hair and beard the growth of fingernails, the forsaking of normal ablutions, living on donated food and having one meal a day.

A Sanyasi was supposed to rise above the requirements of normal material life and devote himself to the seeking of truth. Persons of any caste and ethnic group could become Sanyasi.

Rebirth (Punarjanma) or transmigration of souls —Karma and Moksha: Hindu religion believes in rebirth and its goal is Moksha, or salvation. When a person dies, his soul passes into another body and again into another body until the soul can be freed from all kinds of imperfections (sin) done in the previous life periods. Moksha is the liberation from rebirth and union with the Supreme Soul.

The Four Purusarthas or goals of life: Dharma, Artha, Kama and Moksha constituted the four goals of life. Dharma stands for religion as well as morality righteousness and duty Artha means attainment of wealth; Karma, sexual pleasure; and Moksha, release from the birth cycle, the final goal that an individual has to strive for.

The Three Paths to Moksha: The attainment of knowledge (Gyan Marga), devotion to god (Bhakti Marga) and the path of action (Karma Marga) are the ways to the real attainment of Moksha the union of the individual with the Supreme Soul.

The concept of Avatar or incarnation: In Hindu religion, the Trinity or three gods-Brahma, Vishnu and Maheshor (Shiva) are very important. Brahma is the creator, Vishnu is the preserver and Shiva is the selective destroyer. They are regarded as the supreme being. The concept of 'Avatara' or descent of God in human form is another aspect of Hindu thought. When problems arise, the god takes the form of a suitable creature (another god, a prophet like being) and solves the problem and then disappears.

Religious Leadership and Intellectual Standpoints

Adi Guru Shankaracharya is the only Hindu spiritual leader who is almost universally accepted in this religion. His philosophical standpoints of *Vedanta* were effective in overshadowing Buddhism on the philosophical and intellectual levels. Shankaracharya hails fair a south Indian Brahmin family and is said to have lived around the eighth century. He seems to have had his basic education in a Gurukula, a traditional monastery where education was imparted in ancient times Shankaracharya continued his studies and discourses for which he traveled throughout India. On the way to institutionalizing Hinduism, he established monasteries (Mutts and Matha) under the charge of bishops (Jagatgurus). He established four such Mutts in different parts of India. Although these institutions could not institutionalize Hinduism on the scale of other religions such as Christianity or Buddhism, they left a lasting mark on the Hindu ecclesiastic organization.

The adherents of the Hindu religion follow various rituals and festivals. In the rural, villages of Nepal, local priests help perform these rituals and festivals. Usually the priests learn to conduct various festivals and rituals from their fathers and pass the knowledge to the next generation. There does not exist any institution where people could get formal academic training in religion. Religion is seldom taught in colleges, which have no departments of religion. However, the only Sanskrit University in the district of Dang, Nepal, and some Sanskrit secondary schools, offer some courses on the practice of Hindu rituals.

Buddhism

Lord Buddha was born in Lumbini, Nepal in 623 BC. His personal name was Siddharth, the son of King Suddhodana of the Shakys dynasty. His mother was Queen Mayadevi. The young prince was raised with every luxury at his command until he left his palace.

The beginning of Buddhism traces back to the birth of Buddha. During that time in the bordering towns of India, the Indian society and its religion were undergoing several transitions. The texts known as the Upanishads reflect the changing religious and philosophical thought of the time. This period was marked by the emergence of a powerful royalty, rich merchants and the growth of monasteries where men and sometimes women could dedicate themselves to a life of meditation and spiritual thought. The factors that influenced the growth of Buddhism the most were:

1. The shift from the performance of sacrifice to personal renunciation.
2. The growth of monasteries supported by wealthy kings and merchants.
3. A questioning of the superior position of the priests in the society.

Siddhartha, confronted with the reality of life and the suffering of mankind, decided to find a solution— way out of this universal suffering. During the early period of his life, after a few years of marriage (he was married at the age of 16 years) and the birth of his first child, Rahul, the 29-years-old Siddhartha left the palace and became an ascetic in search of solutions for al kinds of miseries.

There are four major events in the life of the Buddha: his birth, renunciation, enlightenment and attainment of eternal bliss (nirvana) after his death.

For six years, the ascetic Siddhartha wandered in the valley of the Ganges, meeting famous religious teachers, studying and following their systems and methods and submitting himself rigorous ascetic practices. They did not satisfy him. So he abandoned all traditional religions and their methods and went his own way. It was thus that one evening, seated under a tree (since then known as the Bodhi-or Bo-tree, "the Tree of Wisdom") on the bank of the river Neranjara at Buddha-Gaya (near Gaya in Bihar, India), at the age of 35, Siddhartha attained enlightenment, after which he was known as the Buddha, "The Enlightened One".

After his enlightenment, Gautam Buddha delivered his first sermon to a group of five ascetics, his old colleagues, in the Deer Park at Isipatana near Benares, India. From that day, for 45 years, he taught all classes of men and women—kings and peasants, Brahmins and outcastes, bankers and beggars, holy men and robbers—without making the slightest distinction between them. He recognized no differences of caste or social groupings, and the way he preached was open to all men and women who were ready to understand and to follow it.

At the age of 80, Buddha passed away in Kusinara in Uttar Pradesh, India.

As time passed, Buddhism developed several schools. Today there are only two main schools of Buddhism. One is Theravada or the system or school of the elders, considered to be the orthodox and original form of Buddhism as accepted and followed mainly in Sri Lanka, Burma, Thailand, Cambodia, Laos, Chittagong (Bangladesh) and Assam (India), and reintroduced in Nepal about a century ago. This school is also known as *Hinayana,* which means "Small Vehicle", a term coined and used by the Mahayanists. The *Mahayana* or "Grest Vehicle," is a form of Buddhism that developed later. Now it is mainly followed in China, Japan, Korea, Tibet, Vietnam, Mongolia and Nepal. Buddhism is also followed in the United States, Europe, Australia and the Soviet Union to some extent.

Buddhism as a Practicing Religion

Profit is the ultimate goal of development in the so-called modern era. Profit involves greed and ill will that foster ignorance. In Buddhism, these are known as the triad of evils. The goal of Buddhism is the eradication of the triad of evils.

Development certainly involves change. But in the name or development, we have lost our pride dignity and culture. For example, while trying to improve agricultural practices, we have been gradually losing soil fertility. Mechanization has adversely affected our traditional labor system. Mutual help and respect have drastically declined. These are the social repercussions or "development". Development focuses on the economic or material aspects, whereas religion emphasizes the moral and spiritual aspects of societal development.

Self-help is the foundation of sustainable development. Buddhism helps only those who help themselves. As has been very rightly said, Buddha is like a doctor who diagnoses the disease and prescribes the medicine. But it is the patient who takes the medicine. It is entirely upto the patient to obey or disobey the doctor. Therefore Buddha says, one is the master of himself—who else could be the other master Man is his own master and no higher being sits in judgment over his destiny Buddhism teaches self-respect. According to Buddha, man's emancipation depends on his own realization of truth, not on the benevolent grace of a god or external powers as a reward for his obedience and good behavior.

It is generally assumed that physical development will automatically lead to spiritual development, which is in most cases not true. Does quantitative growth automatically lead to peace and fulfillment? Buddhist philosophy says that one's livelihood should be honorable, blameless and harmless to others If this is so, one could question whether the present day development is leading us to a harmless, peaceful and harmonious society. Development should require an abstention from earning a living in anyway that harms others.

Furthermore Buddha guides us in the proper use of our income in the following way (Sugandha Class Note, 1997):

1. One-fifth of one's earning is used to make oneself, one's parents, children, wife and workmen happy and live in comfort.
2. One-fifth is used to share this happiness and comfort with one's friends.
3. One-fifth is used to make oneself secure against all misfortune.
4. One-fifth is used to make the fivefold offering:

   To relatives by giving help to them.

   To guests by welcoming them.

   To the departed by dedicating merit to hem

   To the king—i.e., to the government—by paying taxes and duties and so on.

   To the duties—i.e., those beings who are worshiped according to one's faith.
5. One-fifth is used to support those monks and spiritual teachers who lead a pure and diligent life.

One must make a note from these teachings that Buddha's main focus is sharing or *dana*. The concept of sharing, which could he in the form of material, physical or spiritual, is pivotal for the modern concept of co-operation and development.

Develpment and Morality: Buddhist Point of Development

Challenging the modern world and the social problems associated with development, religious authorities in many Buddhism countries are speaking out on a variety of contemporary social and economic issues. It included the increasing gap between the rich and the poor in the developing world, the exploitation of women in the workplace and as prostitutes, the scourge of AIDS, and the destruction of the natural environment. In a practical sense, the monastery served local communities as school, orphanage, nursing home for the elderly, bank pharmacy, and counseling center.

Looking at all these developments based on Buddhism it is obvious that Buddhist way of development emphasizes the principle of Sammajana or goad individual which will lead to Sammasamaj or good society. Development from a Buddhist perspective visualizes equality, love, freedom and liberation as the ultimate goals. A Buddhist community—be it a village or a nation—would work for harmony and for awakening by getting rid of selfishness of any kind—be it greed hated or delusion. Such development would entail truth beauty, and goodness—be it big or small. Definitely the material development will succeed only with moral development as its foundation. Development without morality is achievement without meaning Morality provides us with a home in order to counter the undesired roots of development which are confusion and madness.

Bikshu Sugandha, 1997, Pokhara.

Buddhism in Nepal

In Buddhism, Buddha was considered mortal. The primary goal was Nirvana. It could be achieved by extinguishing avarices, As the means to this end, the Buddha prescribed a disciplinary eightfold path: to be followed in company with other disciplines. In the third century B.C., the Theravada communities in the Kathmandu Valley joined the adherents of a new doctrine, Mahaysna (Great Vehicle) Buddhism. Tantric Buddhism was known in the Kathmandu Valley by the seventh century A.D. (Lichchavi inscriptions). By the end of the 12th century, a change came to Buddhism, and monasticism started to decline. Hindus and Buddhists were slowly becoming a single caste-oriented community that conformed to Hindu social tradition.

Then another change came into these societies. Highly respected Brahmin priests, Vajracharya and Sakya-bhiksu, began to marry. The Vajracharyas commanded the highest rank in the religious aristocracy if they confirmed their status by the obsenance of the proper initiation rites. The Buddhist community essentially became a formally caste, structured counterpart of the Hindu one, with caste automatically conferred by heredity. Shakya assisted the Vajracharya and both of these groups gained hereditary caste like status. The destruction of viharas in India by Muslims made people move to Kathmandu and to shelter in viharas. About the mid-l4th century under state coercion the Buddhist community began to drift progressively into the Hindu fold. The exception was King Siddhinarasimha Malla (A.D.1619-1661), who did not sanction repression of the Buddhist faith. He himself built new viharas, offered homage to Buddhist divinities and was an ardent devotee of Avalokitesvara in the form of Rato Matsyendranath.

Buddhism survived in the Kathmandu valley until the end of the Malla period because of the benign influence of Tibetan Buddhism. By the 17th century, Tibet had become the holy Buddhist land. During the king Pratap Malla's rule, Newar traders from Kathmandu Valley began to travel regularly to and from Lhasa and to even settle there and in Kuti. The majority the traders were of Manandhers, Tamrakars, Tuladhars, Chitrakars, Kansakars and so on, were traditionally lay Buddhists. Their casteless structure in Tibet had an influence in Kathmandu. This homecoming revitalized the doctrine and almost-forgotten ideas respecting casteless social organization and the Buddhists' respected role in society. This operated as powerful brake and deterrent to the Buddhist drift into Hinduism. They also brought with them Tibetan artifacts. Throughout the Malla period, new viharas and stupas were constructed, and the new Buddhist cult rose and flourished. Even Siddhinarasimha Malla moved, rather than destroyed, a vihara in the path of his expanding palace. During the Malla period, in the late 16th century, two-thirds of the Newars were Buddhists (Regmi, 1999). Tantric manifestations were already in practice- Jamuna Guvaju was the great Tantric of this era.

Buddhist Philosophy in a Nutshell

Teachings of Buddha

There are four noble truths. They are: there is suffering; there is a cause of suffering; there is a cessation or suffering; and there is a way to bring about for the cessation of suffering.

The eight folds paths to the cessation of suffering are; right faith right resolve; right speech; right action; right living; right effort; right thought; and right concentration.

There is the doctrine of dependent origination. Buddhism believes in a theory of a cause and effect. We see an effect only because something has happened. That is to say, an act gives rise to an effect. This doctrine seeks the cause of suffering and the way to stop suffering. Buddhist philosophy believes that, ultimately, ignorance is the cause of suffering and knowledge is the way to end ignorance.

School of Buddhism

There are mainly three schools of Buddhism. Their key features are given below. **Hinayana (Smaller vehicle).** Saying of elders is duly regarded. The main scripture is the tripitaka. Its goal is nirvana (salvation). The ideal saint is Arhat. There should be a personal effort for liberation. There is a concept of God. And there are rules for the followers.

Mahayana (Greater vehicle): There is a concept of the greater vehicle or big ship. Nirvana is not the cessation of misery but a state of bliss. Budhisatwa is the idea saint. Budhisatwa works for others and teaches compassion, love and kindness. Lord Buddha is worshipped. In this school, there is a concept of God and incarnation. It is spread in Tibet, China, Korea, Laos, Vietnam.

Vajrayana (Vehicle of thunder bolt): This school was introduced in the 10 century in India. Vajra stands for symbol of power (Shakti). Tantra and mantra are practiced. There is a belief in magical power. Tara (spouses of Budhisatwa) is the main divinity. The way to salvation is relatively easier.

3

Festivals of Nepal

Buddha Purnima

Date: Buddha Purnima or Buddha Jayanti, the birth anniversary of the Buddha, is widely celebrated in Nepal, on a full moon night in the month of Baisakh (April/May) The Buddha achieved enlightenment as well as nirvana on the same date. Prince Siddharth or Buddha was born in the month of Vaisakh in 563 B.C. It is also believed that Yashodara, Siddharth's wife, his charioteer, Channa, and even his horse, Kantaka, were born on the same day.

Legend: Prince Siddhartha was born in Lumbini in the Rupandehi district of western Nepal after his mother dreamt of a divine light entering her womb. Siddhartha was sheltered from the trials and pains or life by his father, but one day the prince went out of the palace with his charioteer Channa, to see the world outside. He saw poverty, disease and death and was deeply moved by these sights. He became restless and tried to seek the truth behind this eternal cycle of life and death. He left his palace, his wife and child and became an ascetic. He searched for the truth and the reason for the misery of mankind. He attained enlightenment under a banyan tree in Bodh Gaya, a small town in Bihar, India.

Practice: On this day Buddhists offer prayers in their temples and monasteries- Lumbini in Rupandehi, Swayambhunath and Bauddha in Kathmandu, Nepal, are the main centers of celebration. Though this is a festival of the Buddhists, it is invariably celebrated by the Hindus too.

Maha Shivaratri

Date: Maha Shivaratri is celebrated generally in the month of February/March.

Legend: On a moonless night in February every year occurs the night of Shiva, the selective destroyer. This is the night when he is said to have performed the Tandava or the dance of creation, preservation and selective destruction.

Practice: Devotees of Shiva fast during the day and maintain a long vigil during night. In temples all across the country, bells ring, sacred texts are chanted and traditional offerings of leaves of the margosa tree *(Bel)* and milk are made to the Shiva linga (phallus); Shiva's sexual organ of heavenly grandeur. According to ancient scriptures, Shiva manifests himself in the form of a huge flaming linga known as Jyotirlinga on Shivratri. It is the duty of every worshipper to worship this linga with at least one *Bel leaf*. Shiva is worshipped as the god of reproduction represented by the phallus. On this day, hundreds of thousands of Sadhus and other devotees also come to Kathmandu to make a pilgrimage to Lord Pashupatinath Temple, which is one of the holiest temples of the Hindus. They make a bonfire and pass a sleepless night praying to Lord Shiva. On this day the devotees smoke marijuana as a blissful gift of Lord Shiva. Devotees of the Shaiva sect believe that they get to a holy place in Kailash (heaven) after their death.

Holi or Fagu (Festival of Colors)

Dates: Fagu, also known as Holi, is celebrated on the day after the full moon in early March every year.

Legend: Originally a festival to celebrate good harvests and fertility of the land, Holi has several traditional links with legends. According to one popular legend, the word "Holi" is derived from the demoness Holika. She was the sister of Hiranyakashyap, a demon king who, having defeated the gods, proclaimed his own supremacy over the universe, Enraged by his son Prahlad's ardent devotion to the god Vishnu, Hiranyakashyap decided to punish him, He took the help or his sister, Holika, who was immune to damage from fire Holika carried Prahlad into the fire but a divine intervention destroyed her and saved Prahlad. Thus, Holi is celebrated to mark the burning of the evil Holika. It is a celebration of the triumph of good over evil and is commemorated by burning huge bonfires on the eve of Holi asks symbolic representation.

This exuberant festival is also associated with the immortal love of Krishna and Radha. The young Krishna would complain to his mother, Yasoda, about why Radha was so fair and he so dark. Yasoda advised him to apply color on Rahha's face and see how her complexion would change.

According to an ancient legend, Shiva was deep in meditation, oblivious to Parvati, the daughter of the Himalaya, who sought his love. Kama (the Indian version of Cupid) shot an arrow towards Shiva, thus disturbing his meditation. Shiva was enraged and destroyed Kama, reducing him to a heap of ashes. Kama was later resurrected by the intercession of parvati. Yet another legend holds that Holi is the same as the female demon Putana, who tried to kill the child Krishna by making him suckle her poisoned breasts. Krishna however, sucked very hard and drained the life out of Putana. Popular legend adds that the body disappeared and the cowherds or Mathura burnt her with an effigy. Since then, Mathura has been the main centre for Holi.

Practice: Holi announces the arrival of spring and the passing of winter. Young and old alike are drenched with colours. On Holi, people are suddenly caught unawares with colors being poured from the terraces and roofs of houses, bursting balloons, or long pistons squirting colored water. People in small groups are seen singing, dancing and throwing colors on each other. They also eat food laced with bhang, an aphrodisiac that leaves one feeling light and happy.

Holi is celebrated throughout Nepal but it is more predominant in Tarai, southern Nepal. Preparations for the festival begin a week ahead. Houses are given a fresh coat or color, beautiful floral designs are drawn at the entrance, and powdered colors and spraying pistons are bought. In earlier days, the colors were extracted from a flower (Palas tree) that blossoms only during this festival. And the pistons were made of bamboo sticks. But now colors are made artificially and pistons made of different materials are available in various designs. Usually people burn the Holika tree on the eve of Holi. A bonfire is lit in the evenings, with an effigy of Holika. Brahmins circle the fire seven times, reciting religious verses. Folklore and dances are performed around the fire to welcome the new season. On the morning of Holi, people have fun with colored water, Men, women and children all participate in this merrymaking. In the evening youngsters play with dry colors and seek elders' blessings.

Apart from the usual fun with colored powder and water. Holi is marked by vibrant processions, which are accompanied by folk songs, dances and a general sense of abandoned vitality. The color, noise and entertainment that accompany the celebration of Holi bear witness to a feeling of oneness and sense of brotherhood. No other festival brings home the lesson of spiritual and social harmony as well as the festival of Holi! Nepal government declares a legal holiday on Fagu Purnima/Holi.

Teej:

Date: This festival falls in the month of Bhadra (September).

Legend: Parvati or Uma, the daughter of Lord Himalaya learns from her girlfriends that her father had arranged her marriage to Vishnu Parvati is distraught because she had always wanted to marry Shiva. Shiva was her husband in one of her previous incarnations as Sati Devi. On her friend's advice, she runs away to a hidden spot by the banks of a river where she makes a sand phallus, Shiva's symbol, and worships it. Shiva notices her devotion and, pleased, grants her a boon. She asks for Shiva as her husband, and her wish is granted (Bennett, 1983).

Practice: Teej is practiced by fasting and worshipping Lord Shiva. All married mostly Hindu women observe fasting, aspiring to a blissful conjugal life, progress and prosperity- for their husbands, a good future for themselves and purification of body and soul. Young and unmarried women also fast and worship Lord Shiva, aspiring for good husbands. For an unmarried woman, compliance with the age-old tradition ensures a good, loving, and caring husband. The fasting women wear red sari and blouse and visit the Shiva temple. It is customary in Nepal that daughters and sisters are invited by their parents and brothers in their homes for good feast on the eve of Teej. All those who fast the next day usually eat good food locally known as *Dar Khane* until the midnight on the eve of Teej.

Early in the morning of Teej, they take baths, worship and fast. Usually those who fast do not even drink water for 24 hours. On Teej the high spirits, flirtatiousness and the sexuality that women must ordinarily suppress are released at shiva's temple. During the daytime, women visit the temple and dance. The songs are usually related to the uncordial relationship between daughters-in law and mothers-in-law. The daughters-in-law describe all sorrows and sufferings that they had faced all the year. Traditionally, Nepal women used to get married at a very early age and Teej would be a rare and good opportunity for them to open the heart. In present day Nepal there is a tendency among the educated rural women to sing politically oriented songs. Either they expose the misdeeds of the government or the political system or describe how exploitation is being nurtured in the feudal society. They also chant religious hymns, recalling the ordeal that Parvati, Shiva's consort, had gone through to win the heart of all living beings. On the second day, usually they take a simple bath, make offerings to a Brahmin and worship before they break their fast. They eat a very simple and purely vegetarian meal. On the third and the last day, which is also known as Rishi Panchami, women who had undergone the fast pay homage to various deities situated on the banks of a sacred river. Bathing on this day is of a special type. They tooth brush with 360 twigs of a special religious plant locally known as *Datiwan*. They also rub all parts of their body with red mud and dip their bodies in the holy water 360 times. It is assumed that this ritual cleans the body and soul from whatever sin they might have committed for the whole year. Women believe that fasting on Teej makes their husbands' lives long. The Teej fasting (*Brat*) concludes after they perform Rishi Puja (worship of Rishi) with the help of a Brahmin priest

Dashain

Dates: Dashain, also known as Vijayadashmi, is celebrated on the tenth day, of Durga Pooja (Nauratha), sometime in October.

Legend, King Rama of Ayodhya. India killed King Ravana of Lanka on this day and hence it is celebrated as the day of victory. Rama invoked the blessings of the divine mother, the goddess Durga, before actually going out to battle.

Practice; Dashai is one of the most important festivals for all the Nepalese and it is celebrated with much joy throughout the country. The first day of Dashai is known as *Ghatasthapana*. On this day, a holy water vessel representing Durga is established and oat seed is sown for its seedlings to be used as "Jamara" on the 10th day. On the eighth day, known as the *kalratri*, animal sacrifices are done at Durga temples. Countless buffalo are sacrificed, which also represent the demon Mahishasur. The ninth day, the last day of Navaratri is known as Maha Navami. For the nine days of Navaratri, the goddess of power-Durga / Kali / Nava Durga—is worshipped. People go to the Kali temples to worship. They also worship in the home. In many houses in the prayer room, barley seeds are sown in an earthen pot or a plate made of leaves on the first day. The seeds are coveted to arrest any light. In nine days, they attain a height of about 5 to 6 inches and develop yellow color. This is a known as *Jamara*. The tenth day is a day of joy and celebration. This was the day when Rama killed Rawana. This is also taken as a victory of virtue over sin. On this day, people lay visit to the elderly for rib and blessing. The tika is made of vermilion powder, rice grain and milk curd (yogurt). The elders bless the youngsters with tika on the forehead and Jamara on the head.

This is the biggest festival for all Hindus of Nepal. It has a great social significance, too. Family reunion is an important part of this festival. Children and adults wear new and fancy clothes on this Occasion. They enjoy good food, too. Government offices are closed for 10 days and most of the schools and universities are closed for 15 days. Employees get one-month salary as a bonus to celebrate this festival.

In several southern districts of Tarai, for 10 days processions depicting various facets of Rama's life are taken out and scenes from his life enacted out in a popular form of drama celled Ramlila. On Vijayadashmi day, colossal effigies of Ravana, his brother, Kumbhkarna, and son, Meghnath, are burnt in vast open spaces by Rama (usually the actor who plays Rama in Ramlila). His consort, Sita, and his brother, Lakshmana who shoots arrows of fire at the effigies, which are stuffed with crackers and firework, accompany him. In burning the effigies, the people are asked to burn the evil within them and thus follow the path of virtue and goodness, hearing in mind the example of Ravana, who despite all his might and majesty was destroyed for his evil behaviors

Diwali / Tihar / Bhaitika (Festival of Lights)

Date: A family festival, it is celebrated 15 days after Vijaya Dashami, on the 13th day of the dark fortnight of the month of Ashwin / Kartik (October / November).

Legend: It is a festival of lights symbolizing the victory of righteousness and the lifting of spiritual darkness. The word

"Deepawli" literally means "rows of clay lamps". This festival commemorates Lord Rama's return to his kingdom Ayodhya after completing his 14-year exile. Another view is that Deepawali is meant to celebrate the destruction of the arrogant tyrant Bali at the hands of Vishnu when the latter appeared in his Vamana (dwarf) avatar.

Practice: Tihar is celebrated for usually five days. Worship of crows, dogs, oxen, cow, the goddess of wealth and the brothers takes place during this period. The third day is one of the important days. Twinkling oil lamps, or diyo, light up every home and fireworks displays are common all across the country. The goddess Lakshmi (consort of Vishnu) who is the symbol of wealth and prosperity is worshiped on the third day. This festive occasion also marks the beginning of ancient Nepal's new year. Houses across the country are scrubbed until they are spotlessly clean and whitewashed with fresh white paint. To enhance their new look, they are decorated with bright paper lanterns, electric lights and flowers, while the girls of the house embellish the Aangan (courtyard) and walls with traditional aesthetic designs and patterns. New clothes are bought and the family gathers together to offer prayer, distribute sweets and light up their homes. Crackers and fireworks illuminate the sky and people pray for prosperity. On this third day, girls in the groups visit their neighbors in the evening, sing and give blessings to the visited. The playing of songs is known as *Bhailo Khelne*. In the evening, the goddess of wealth is worshipped. In every house, usually the woman heal of the household puts all ornaments (jewelry) and a new bundle of currency in front of the goddess and all worships together. All the pathways art cleaned and lights and doors are kept open, hoping that the goddess of wealth will visit the home and bless it with lot of wealth. On the fourth day, groups or boys visit their neighbors and sing the songs and bless the visited. The song is locally known as *Deusiri Khelne*. Among the Newar community, the fourth day of Tihar has a special significance. On this auspicious day, all the family members sit together, wear clean clothes and worship themselves. This is known as *Ma Puja*, meaning worshipping of oneself.

The fifth and last day is known as Bhai Tika. "Bhai" in Nepali stands for "brother"? On this day, all sisters worship their brothers and brothers and sisters bless each other. The brothers offer gifts to their sisters. Tihar is also called *Panchak Yama*. Yama is the god of death. According to one of the Hindu legends, a queen had brought back the life of her king by worshipping Yama. Similarly, sisters on that day while worshipping make their brothers sit together and make a boundary line of oil with doob grass. There is a belief that no one, even death, can cross the boundary line and thus the sisters guard the life of their brothers. During the five days, they will be offering good food to all those who are associated with Yama- i.e., the dog, crow, oxen and the cow. The sister's worship is for the longevity and prosperity of their brothers. This is an exceptionally joyful occasion for the married sisters to express their love and affection for their natal home. They usually invite their brothers into their own homes turn by turn to eat during the other days.

Id-Ul-Fitr (Ramazan Id)

Dates: Coming with the new moon, this festival marks the end of Ramazan, the ninth month of the Muslim year, and is celebrated in April / May.

Legend: It was during this month that the holy Koran was revealed.

Practice: Nepal Muslims keep a fast every day during this month, and on the completion of the period, which is decided by the appearance of the new moon, Id-ul-Fitr is celebrated with great eclat. Prayers are offered in mosques and Idgahs and elaborate festivities are held.

Muharram

Dates: Muharram is not a festival in the celebratory sense—it mourns the Karbala tragedy when Imam Husain, grandson of Prophet Muhammad, was martyred in the 61st year of the Hijra (A.H.). It takes place during the first month of the Muslim calendar in August / September. It is observed in different ways in various parts of Nepal, but the theme of mourning is constant throughout.

Legend: After the death of the Prophet, questions of succession arose. There could be no successor of the spiritual head, because Islam believes in the finality of Muhammed in the prophetic tradition. After him, the Koran was considered the final word in revelations and settlement of disputes and conflicts. However, a successor to the position of caliph was needed. Muhammed had named no successor and had only one daughter, Fatimah, who was married to Ali, and had two children-Hassan and Hussein. One camp believed that succession should remain within Mohammed's family, while another disagreed. Finally. Abu Bakr, a loyal follower of Muhammed, was elected caliph. His reign was peaceful, as was that of his successors. However, during the reign of Ali, there was major opposition from the masses, and as a result of the aggression, Ali was assassinated. His son Hassan was poisoned, while his other son Hussein was killed in the battle of Karbala. This tragic circumstance divided the Muslim community into sects - the Shiahs and the Sunnis. The Shiahs consider Ali, Hassan and Hussein the rightful caliphs and publicly mourn their death during Muharram.

Practice: Profusely decorated taziyas (bamboo and paper replicas of the martyr's tomb), embellished with gilt and mica, as well as green alams (standards of Hazrat Imam Hussain's army) made of: silver, copper and brass, are carried through city streets. A horse is led in the procession in memory of Hussain's horse Dul Dul. Wrestlers and dancers enact Scenes depicting the battle at Karbala. Every day, marsiyars (mourning verses) are recited in honour of the martyred, as young men beat their breasts, crying "Husain! Husain!" in collective sorrow. On the 10th day, The processions carrying the taziyas and alams are called Ashura. They terminate in open spaces called Imambaras, where the taziyas are buried, or in the local burial ground known as the Karbala.

This historical event is observed with great passion particularly in the western districts of Nepal, as it is the center of Shia culture and religious activities, and accordingly a large number of taziyas and the alams are taken out all over the villages and towns. In the villages, people even wear black and celebrate the festival with grandeur. It has been usually found that taziyas are made and brought in this occasion from those houses where there had been a death within one year. Sometimes Hindu neighbous also follow this practice in Nepali Tarai villages where the Muslim population is significant.

4

Tibetan Buddhism in Nepal

Just over two decades ago The American writer Peter Mathiessen travelled to the remote Monastery of Shey Gompa, deep in the Tibetan-speaking region of Dolpo on Nepal's frontier with Tibet. It was a remarkable journey, a pilgrimage both physical and spiritual, resulting in the publication of a literary classic, which successfully blends two disparate *genres*-travel and philosophy—in a single journey of discovery to one of the last bastions of free Tibetan culture.

Today few people are permitted to journey to the fastness of Dolpo. The region has been made part of Shey-Phoksundo, Nepal's largest national park, and the monastery of Shey Gompa lies beyond the restricted inner line, Besides, the journey entails many days hard trekking over some of the highest passes in Nepal, before the high mountain deserts of the Tibetan plateau are eventually reached. Few people, moreover, have the time inclination and stamina to follow literally in Matthiessen's footsteps; for most a figurative journey, via The pages of his book will have to suffice.

That said, there are several more readily accessible regions of Nepal where the vital essence of Tibetan culture can be experienced, albeit not in the pristine setting of Shey Gompa, abode of The itinerant snow leopard and perhaps—who knows?—the yeti. One such is Bodhnath, also known as Baudha, the largest and most important Tibetan Buddhist monument outside Tibet.

Set squarely in the *siddhi*—a zone of supernatural power where guardian deities dwell and wishes are granted—Bodhnath is located just six kilometres east of Kathmandu, along the long, old trade road to Lhasa. Known to the Tibetans simply as *Chorten Chempo,* or "Great Stupa", it has been the Mecca of Tibetans in exile ever since the Chinese occupation of their homeland in 1950. Bodhnath has also developed as a centre for the study of Tibetan Buddhism, numerous monasteries having been built in effective replacement of those destroyed by Mao Tse-tung's Red Guards

Throughout the area many Tibetans are also involved in more worldly activities, ranging from selling handicrafts and souvenirs, through dry goods, to running food stalls and restaurants. Whether seeking spiritual enlightenment, a deeper understanding of Tibetan culture and politics, or a first taste of *chang*, fermented Tibetan corn beer-' Bodhnath is the appropriate place to go. Dusk is, perhaps, the best time to visit. The tourist buses will have departed, and the resonant chanting of monks blends strangely but well with the unfamiliar rhythms of gongs, cymbals and Tibetan stringed instruments. Pilgrims shuffle and prostrate their way around the great stupa, seemingly unobserved by the high cheek-boned, rosy-faced merchants who squat in the doorways of their establishments drinking endless cups of salted yak-butter tea—an acquired taste if ever there was one!

The origins of Bodhnih are lost in the mists of time, but tradition fixes the foundation in the fifth century AD. According to legend, a daughter of the god Indra stole flowers from heaven, and was punished by being reborn the daughter of a poor poultry farmer in a Kathmandu Valley village. To atone for her earlier crime, she lived a blameless life, becoming prosperous enough to build a gigantic stupa at Bodhnath to honour Amitabha, the Buddha of the past age. Whatever truth lies behind this legend, Tibetians attach great importance to it for it goes on to warn of an invasion of their homeland by a powerful enemy, which would scatter the Tibetans southwards into Nepal and India. In 1950, when China occupied Tibet and more particularly in 1959, when the Dalai Lama fled from Lhasa to Dharamsala, this prophecy seemed finally to have been borne out.

Today the great dome of Bodhnath looms high over the surrounding monasteries, easily visible from several kilometres distance. With a diameter and a height of forty metres, it is easily the largest sacred structure in the valley. The massive base, looking rather like an inverted alms bowl, supports a four-sided, fourteen-stepped, gilded spire, which in turn is topped by a gilded, crown-shaped *harmika*- Prayer flags, hung from tautly-stretched hemp ropes, snap and flutter in the cold breath of the Himalayas. But it is the all-seeing eyes, which give Bodhnath its particular appeal. Painted in black, ochre and white, with pale blue irises, they seem watchful - almost menacing - and certainly not of this world. It is as though a giant visage was peering from the centre of the stupa, never-sleeping, ever-vigilant, and staring... straight at you.

The all-seeing eyes of Bodhnath

To the first Christian missionaries in the Vale of Kathmandu, as to the armies of the Mogul ruler Shams-ud-Din Ilyas who briefly captured the valley at the beginning of the 13th century, the all-seeing eyes of Bodhnath must have seemed the very epitome of idolatry, numinous with the power of false religion and—we may be sure—an object of fear and dread- Certainly the Muslim forces of Shans-ud-Din destroyed many of the finest monuments in the region including the nearby Hindu temple of Pashupatinath, and we maybe sure that Bodhnath, too, suffered the wrath of the iconoclast.

Happily, today, such is no longer the case. Over the centuries Kathmandu Valley has attained a level of communal tolerance, with Hindu and Buddhist, Muslim and Christian living peacefully, side-by-side. Yet Bodhnath retains its power to inspire feelings of awe, regardless of religious persuasion, in all who see it. A narrow passage provides entrance to the sacred area, which is dominated by the colossal bulk of the whitewashed stapa, rising up to the all-seeing eyes. The gilded spire, set against the brilliant blue Himalayan sky, induces a sense of the transience and insignificance of the individual self. Buddhist pilgrims perform the pradakshina, or clockwise circumambulation of the stupa, to the sound of chanting monks and the soft whir and gentle rumble of Buddhist prayer wheels, each inscribed with the eternal mantra so elegantly elucidated by Matthiessen.

The deep, resonant *Om* is all sound and silence throughout time, the roar of eternity and also the great stillness of pure being... The Mani is the "adamantine diamond" of the Void-the primordial, pure and indestructible essence of existence... **Padme** is the world of phenomena, samsara, unfolding with spiritual progress to reveal beneath the leaves of delusion the jewel of nirvana. **Hum** has no literal meaning... Perhaps it is simply a rhythmic exhortation completing the mantra.

This is the very core of Bodhnath, Lord of Eternal, Universal Wisdom, and spritual heart of Tibetan Buddhism in Nepal.

Prayer wheels

Close by the main stupa other temples cluster. In the past fifteen years, as Tibetan Buddhists have gained new confidence in the wake of Chinese invasion and Red Guard destruction of their homeland, several new *gompa*, or monasteries, have been built. Most have been deliberately named after *gompo* in Tibet that have been destroyed by The Chinese. Today there are more than a dozen in the immediate neighbourhood, and Bodhnath has emerged as a major centre of Tibetan Buddhist scholarship, attracting students from all over the world.

One reason for Bodhnath's appeal is the presence of maroon-robed monks from all four major Tibetan Buddhist sects, encouraging an atmosphere of debate and the easy exchange of ideas. This contrasts with the Tibetan "capital-in-exile" of Dharamsala in India, where some students feel the politically charged atmosphere detracts from spiritual study, and where the *Gelug-pa* or "Yellow Hat" order of the Dalai Lama predominates over other sects. Still, links between Bodhnath and Dharamsala are strong; The Cini Lama, Third highest dignitary of the Tibetans after the Dalai Lama and the Panchen Lama, resides at Bodhnath, and comings and goings between the two centres are many and often.

The older monasteries clustered around Bodhnath keep their doors open most of the time, and visitors are welcome to attend morning and evening services. Here, besides the *Gelug-pa*, it is possible to observe followers of the *Nyingma-pa*, or "Red Hat!! sect, the oldest Tibetan order, dating back to the eighth century AD, as well as adherents of the intermediate orders, *Sakya-pa* and *Kagyu-pa*. Whatever The sect, The structure and lay-out of the various monasteries are broadly similar. Gilded statues representing the Buddha, various bodhisattvas, and the thunder of the particular sect occupy places of honour in the main hall. Spread out in front of these will be butter-fuelled lamps, which monks and pilgrims constantly replenish, as well as offerings of incense, flowers, food and money. On the smoke-darkened walls lovingly executed frescos portray the four temple guardians or express the complex cosmology of Tibetan Buddhism.

At Bodhnath, despite the continuing tragedy of their homeland, Tibetan culture and religious beliefs continue to flourish beneath the approving gaze of the all-seeing eye.

Om! The Jewel in the Heart of the Lotus. *Hum*!

Buddhism in Nepal

The dictum of Gautama Buddha, soon after his enlightenment, "Wander forth, Ye O Monks, for the good of many, for the happiness of many" seems to have inspired his disciples to propagate the religion so much that they went to the furthest length to spread the teachings of Buddhism through-out its long career. The teaching of Sakyamuni was meant for all men irrespective of caste, creed, sex, social status or state of civilization. Within India, Buddhism could not obtain full scope on account of the hold of the Brahmanas on the common people, hide-bound, as they were, by the caste (varna) and ritualistic system of the Brahmanas. There were several erudite Brahmanas, with a spiritual and philosophical bent of mind, who could see through the artificiality of *varna*-system and ritualism, eschewed their inherited faith and religion and joined the Buddhist Sangha in order to derive the full benefit of the deep teachings of Gautama Buddha.

The lay-society appreciated the self-sacrificing spirit of the Buddhist monks, and satisfied themselves by just making donations as much as they could afford to the Sangha, with or without the hope of earning merits. The Buddhist monk-preachers, not finding a very fruitful field for conversion among the masses of India, directed their attention to the peoples living in and outside the borders of India, where Brahmanic caste-system and ritualism could not cast its influence.

The tribal people had a culture of their own with animistic beliefs, spirit-worship, etc. To them the missionaries despatched during the reign of Asoka directed their attention and proceeded to the frontiers of India or the countries beyond. One of the missionaries was Majjhima, who went to the Himalayan region along with Kassapagotha, relics of both of whom have been discovered in a relic-urn at Sanchi with the inscription of the names on the lid and described as "Hemavatacariya".

In the Nagarjunikonda inscription, there is a reference to the atempt for spreading the religion in Cina-Cilate, of which Cilata is dentified with the Kiratas living in the eastern Himalayan region, that is the frontier of Nepal, the vasts forest adjoining Lumbini Spread of Buddhism took place in its very early stage during the times of Asoka and Kanishka in Ceylon on the south and in the N.W. Frontiers of India, including Afghanistan, Balkh and Bamiyan, Central Asia and Nepal in the north. The ancient Kiratas were the earliest people of Nepal to receive the teachings of Buddhism, evidently in its elementary form, which was mixed in with their animistic and other beliefs. They were followed by the Licchavis arid Newars, both of which tribes, particularly the Newars, became Buddhist but they did not eschew altogether their ancient religion, *Saivism*.

Thoughout the history of Nepal up to the modern times, the people in general adored both Saiva and Buddhist deities and hence, the form of Buddhism prevailed here all along was neither pure Hinayana nor Mahayana nor Tantrayana. The latest rulers of Nepal, the Gurkhas, though staunch Sivaite, were tolerant of Buddhism. All the earlier ruling dynasties and the people in general, were either Sivaites or Buddhists but worshipped the deites of both the religions, and extended their patronage to both of them, sometimes, identifying Siva with Buddha, and Brahma with Adibuddha, the Svayarnbhu, i.e. the self-existent, unborn and undecaying, the deified form of Dharmakaya, the universe or Sunyata.

Nepal, however, is the only country, which preserved the most valuable treasures of Indian Buddhism, that is, the original manuscripts of Mahayana and Tantrayana literature, which became known to Indian and European scholars through the efforts of a great scholar B.B. Hodgson. Quite a number of these manuscripts or their copies were taken to Sa-skya and other monasteries of Tibet, and formed the bases of Tibetan Kanjur and Tanjur. The Banepa-kuti pass of Nepal leading to Tibet served as one of the routes for transmission of Indian Buddhism to Tibet, and the mutual contact of Indian and Tibetan savants. Both Indian and Nepalese monks of Odantapuri and Vikramasila, including the famous apostle Atisa, reached Tibet through Nepal.

The great Tibetan king Srong-btsan-sgam-po and his successors ruled not only over Tibet but also extended their dominion to some portions of Nepal and Central Asia. This political relation paved the way for the propagation of Buddhism in these two countries. The famous scholar Thon-mi-sambhota developed the Tibetan script out of the Gupta style of script prevailing in Kashmir and Nepal. Hence, Buddhism of Nepal was the product of both Indian and Tibetan missionaries. The contributions of Tibet to the Nepalese stupas of Svayambhunath and Budhnath were no less than tose of the Nepalese rulers. From the stupas and divinities worshipped in Nepal, it may be inferred that the latest phase of Buddhism, Tantrism became popular in Nepal as also in Tibet. This was also due to the efforts of the missionaries of Odantaupri and Vikramasila. Further, in the eastern sub-Himalayan region of Nepal, the original inhabitants belonged to the Tibetan stock and they are still living in this area, adhering to both Bon-po and Buddhist faith.

In this article, it is proposed to reconstruct a history of Nepalese Buddhism, on the basis of the tribes and rulers, who patronised, and devoted themselves to, the religion, preceded by a topographical and tribal sketch of Nepal, and concluded with an account of the two stupas Svayam-bhunath and Budhnath.

Topography

Nepal is situated on the southern slopes of the Himalayas extending up to the Indo-Gangetic plains. At the earliest period the country of Nepal denoted only the valley of Kathmandu with its length and breadth about 100 miles on each direction and was about 60 miles north of the Indo-Gangetic plain. The valley of Nepal was late-extended to the south by the inclusion of the large forests of the Terai reaching up to the border of India. On the east, it extended over the mountainous region up to the borders of Tibet and Sikkim. On the west, it extended up to Kumaun. Its present area is about 50,000 square miles with a population of about 8 millions.

Tribes

The original inhabitants of Nepal were many tribes of the Indo-Mongoloid stock. The main population consisted of the Kiratas Licchavis and Newars, many of whom became intermingled and became known as Newars. They were surrounded by Magar, Gurungs, Son-wars, Kachars, Limbus, Lepchas, Kasundas and Murmis. The physiognomy of all these different tribal peoples shows a fairly close affinity. The ancient language was mainly that of the Newars who were the best-cultured people of the country.

Kiratas

The Kiratas were the earliest Himalayan tribe to come to Nepal and to settle down there. They included the clans of Khambus, Limbus, Tharus and a few others. The Kiratas are mentioned in as early as a Vedic Text: the White Yajurveda (Vajasaneyi samhita), in the two Epics, Manava-dharma-sastra, Bharavi's Kiratarjuniyam and Peri-plus. In the Epics, they are mentioned along with Sakas, Yavanas and Pallavas. They fraternised with Cinas under Bhagadatta, the king of Kamarupa (Prag-jyotisa). In the Lalita-Vistara, one of the forms of writing mentioned is Kirata-lipi. In the Nagariunikonda inscription referred to above, they are associated with Cina with the name Cilata. In the Milindapanha (p.322) is mentioned Cina-vilata of which "Vilata" seems to be a misreading for Cilata. Dr. Regmi says that the were living in Balkh and Dardistan. Prof. Levi writes that Cilata was a of Mahacina which included Nepal.

There is the tradition that the Kiratas were originally Ksatriyas but for non-compliance with the prescribed duties-obligations of their caste, they were degraded to Sudras. Buddhism had already spread to Balkh and Dardistan and so they must have known of Buddhism before they entered into Nepal. They took possession of the eastern valley of Nepal 5 or 6 days journey from Bhatgaon and ruled there for 29 generations i.e. for about 725 years. While in the Buddhist territories they muttered Om Mani Padme Hum and gave presents to Lamas but while in Hindu area they worshipped Siva and Gauri and made gifts to Brahmanas.

Licchavis

The Licchavis of Vaisali, situated in close proximity to Nepal, after losing their independence in India entered into Nepal conquered the Kiratas and settled down in the country. They ruled for about six centuries from the 1st century A.D. Jayadeva was their first ruler. These Licchavis were different from those, who live in the days of Sakyamuni, and perhaps belonged to the clan, with whom the Guptas rulers, Chandragupta I and Samudragupta had relations. Like the Gupta rulers, the Licchavis were worshippers of Siva and Visnu. Among the Licchavi rulers, Narendradeva, Sivadeva and Puspadeva became ardent supporters of Buddhism. Narendradeva's regared for Buddhism is shown in some of his inscriptions by the representation of the symbol of the Buddhist wheel of law (*Dharmacakra*) flanked by two deer. It is said that Narendradeva though Sivaite, always kept an image of Buddha with him as a magical charm.[8] In his old age, he retired to a Buddhist monastery, and at the time of his death he gave to his son, his crown along with a copy of the Prajnaparamita.

In the *Manjusrimulakalpa*, appears the following passage "There will be in Nepal in the north in the Himalayan region a king of the Licchavi dynasty. He will be very prosperous on account of his attaining perfection in Mantras known as Bhogavarti. He will reign for 80 years in a kingdom bereft of thieves." Very likely the king referred to in this passage is Narendradeva. "There will be many other kings of this dynasty who will worship the famous Taradevi clad in white who renders untiringly and at all times help to all". It may be mentioned here that Vajra-yogini, Ugra-Tara and Nila-Tara were and are being worshipped by the Nepalese Buddhists.

In the Yagbahal inscription of Sivadeva II (8th Century A.D.) after mentioning the name of Licchavi-kulaketu Paramabhattaraka Maharajadhirala Narendradeva, is recorded that a grant was made to the fraternity of monks of the four quarters. A monastery was built by king Sivadeva who named it as "Sivadeva-vihara-catur-dig-bhikhu-sanghasya." During the reign of Lichavi-kula-ketu Puspadeva further grants were made to the monks of Sivadeva-vihara. In this inscription are mentioned incidentally a few other monasteries viz. Manadeva-vihara Gupta-vihara, Kharjurikavihara, Abhayakavi-vihara, Raja-vihara and Saciva-vihara. King Bhaskaradeva erected also a few monasteries viz., Hiranya vihara, Mahavihara and Pingala-vihara. Besides, the above, there were also many other monasteries, some of which were known as Varta-kalyana-vihara, Catur-bhalankasana-vihara and Sriraja-vihava.[12]

Most of these monasteries had extensive land-grants, known as Agraharas, which the donees enjoyed free of all taxes and revenues payable to the State. The object of such grants, as is described in the inscriptions was to encourage learning and spiritual practices of monks by keeping them above cares and anxieties for the bare necessaries of life as also to see that the viharas grew into centres of education and cultural progress.

Inspite of their Saiva faith, the later Licchavi rulers not only made lavish grants to Buddhist monasteries but also had great regared for Buddhism and Buddhist monks, e.g. king Jayadeva and his queen worshipped Avalokitesvara.

The kings also encouraged the propagation of Buddhist literature as is proved by their affixing signatures to many manuscripts. Mention may be made of the signatures of Narendradeva in a copy of the Prajnaparamita in Sri-vihara, of Baladeva in a copy of the Saddharmapundarika and of Sankara deva in Astasahasrika Prajnaparamita and Bodhicaryavatara.

It lies to the credit of Narendradeva, to establish closer contact with Tibet through the Banepa-kuti Pass (Bhotta in Tibetan) said to the shortest route from China and Tibet to India. Mahayana Buddhism was introduced into Tibet some time before Santiraksita and admasambhava by Buddhist missionaries resididing in Nepal, along with the Pagoda Style of architecture of temples. Both artists and missionaries of Nepal contributed much to the cultural advancement of Tibet in the first half of the 7th Century A.D.

Mallas

11th to 14th Century A.D.

The Mallas, according to Prof. Tucci, were the Khasiyas of Simla and Garhwal. Their conquest and rulership of the area from Western Nepal to Western Tibet were discovered by Prof. Tucci in his latest expedition to Nepal, 1953. Nagadeva conquered Western Tibet in the 12th Century while Prthivi Malla was the last ruler of this dynasty, when Western Tibet regained its independence. These Malla rulers were perhaps tolerant of Buddhism, as one of its rulers bearing the name of Asoka made a donation to the temple of Bodh Gaya. The Mallas were originally Hindus, but on the top of the steles, discovered by Prof. Tucci at Dullu and in the neighbouring villages containing the genealogy of the Malla rulers, appears a Buddhist symbol with the inscription "Om Mani Padme Hum" The Mallas, while in Tibet, became Buddhist and built the magnificent temples of Tsaparang and Toling, discovered by Prof. Tucci in his expedition in 1931-33. They used Tibetan language in the north and Sanskrit in the south of their dominion. Prof. Petech utilizing the colophons of Nepalese mss, in which the names of kings with their dates are usually given by the copyists, compiled a chronological history of the Malla rulers with Arimalla as the first to reign in Nepal in 1200 A.D. They were mainly Saivas and had no connection with Buddhism. There is no indication in this chronology how these Malla kings were related to the Malla rulers, whose genealogy was discovered by Prof Tucci at Dullu. Prof. Tucci writes that the latest Malla rulers of Nepal were different from the Mallas whose genealogy, he had discovered at Dullu.

Newars

The Newars were a composite race of Indo-Mongoloid origin. Being the first settlers and the oldest inhabitants of the valley of Kathmandu, they absorbed many tribal peoples who came to live in the valley. They had close affinity to Magars, Gurungs, Lepchas, Sonwars, Kachars, Murmis, Limbus and Kiratas. Their language was Indo Mongoloid and not Indo-Aryan, though they absorbed much of Indian culture. They might have some relations with the Vrji clan of Vaisali They were the first people of Nepal among whom the Buddhist evangelist. made their attempts to propagate the teachings of Buddhism. In Chinese there is a tradition that Bodhisattva Manjusri opened out a passage for the water encompassed and locked in Nepal and converted it into a habitable country. His companions were the Newars, Who first colonised the country. They ruled over the valley of Kathmandu for about 725 years up to the advent of the Gurkhas. They along with other tribes shared the territory with the changing ruling tribes including the Gurkhas who ruled over Nepal from 1768.

The Newars were excellent craftsmen, made beautiful bronze images and painted figures. They made graceful images of Buddha Avalokitesvara or Padmapani, as also of the Divine Mercy but in various demonaic forms. They were not only artists but also architects. They introduced the Pagoda Style of architecture in temples of both Nepal and Tibet. There were among them learned men and the most learned among them were given the highest place in the caste distinction, which was later imposed on them by the Brahmanic influence.

Buddhism as is well known deprecated strongly the caste-system, which made an artificial distinction of high and low among human beings. The various tribes absorbed in Indian population were generally relegated to a lower caste. The Buddhist evangelists preferred to work among the hill-people who were not obsessed with caste-distinctions. There were divisions among them according to professions and tribal origins. The Buddhist monks found the Newars of Nepal, a composite tribal people, suitable for propagating their religion and received good response from them. The Newars also adapted their habits, customs and practices to the teachings of Buddhism but with the advent of Brahmanic influence, particularly the Saivites, who became rulers of the land, the Newars had to submit themselves to a special caste-distinction on lines similar to those of the Brahmanic system. The Sivivamargis were generally the ruling class, while the common people were Buddhamargis. caste system in Nepal came into vogue both among the Hindus as well as the Buddhists in the reign of the Thakuris but was made more and more rigid during the reign of Jayasthiti Malla in the 14th century A.D. Intermarriage between different castes became restricted and two sets of caste-distinction were introduced in the two religious groups: Sivamargi and Buddhamargi.

The monks who formerly led a celibate life claimed that they were descendants of India Brahmanas and Ksatriyas and as such they were of the highest castes. They took advantage of the Brahmanic form of married priesthood and started marrying and having families and, at the same time, earning their livelihood by officiating as priests of the Buddhists and enjoying the yield of the monastic properties. The caste system of the Newars or the common people in general was made thus:-

I Vajracarya or Gubhaju-learned monks;

II Sakya-bhiksu (Bandya-Banra) -monks without much learning and many taking up profession of goldsmith;

III Sresthas: Kayastha (scribes), Nikhu (painter of images of deities), Lakhay (attendants);

IV (a) Lower castes, corresponding to Sudras. They are Uday or Urag (merchants) Carpenters, Metal workers.

(b) Jyapu (cultivators)

(c) All sorts of manual workers engaged in various trades and professions and

V Untouchables.

The above list indicates broadly the form of caste distinction of the Buddhamargis. Of these the Vajracarya-Sakyabhiksu replaced the Buddhist monks but retained the formalities of ordination in a strong manner.

Ordination of a Newari Buddhist Priest

Prof. Levi has given an account of the whole procedure of ordination of a Newari Buddhist priest. Buddhism underwent a revolutionery change in Nepal along with the ceremony of ordination retaining just a few formalities of the ancient ceremony. The Bandyas (Banras) are only entitled to ordination, which, however, was not given to one who married and became the father of a family and took the profession of an artisan. The Bandyas could be given ordination before their marriage, and only the ordained Bandyas could be the officiating priests. The procedure of ordination is as follows:-

A candidate seeking ordination with a view to qualify himself for becoming officiating priest, approaches a spiritual preceptor (Guru) and requests him to give him ordination.

The Guru, before commencing the actual ceremony, draws a magical diagram and utters spells for giving protection to the candidate from three dangers, viz,. from thunderbolt, iron and fire. The spells are known as Vajraraksa, Loharaksa and Agniraksa.

The candidate is then sprinkled with a jar of consecrated Water. This ceremony is known as *Kalasa-abhiseka*.

Two days later the Guru who is usually the head (*Nayaka*) of a monastery and four senior priests of other monasteries, i.e. five priests in all, as was the ancient custom, confer the vow of renunciation from worldly life (*Pravrajya-vrata*) on the candidate along with the prescription for observance of five moral precepts (*Siksapadas*) viz., non-killing, non-stealing, celibacy, and abstention from falsehood and intoxicating drinks.

The next step is that the candidate is to get himself shaved of hair, moustache and beard. He is then given a religious name and is sprinkled with consecrated water. He is asked to observe five additional precepts i.e. ten siksapadas in all, viz, abstention from enjoying dances, from use of ornamental articles, from sleeping on high bed, form taking food beyond fixed time, and from touching gold and silver.

The candidate is then asked to put on the robes of a monk (*civare*) and under-garment (*nivasa*), and to take a begging bowl (*pindapatra,*) a stick (*khikkhari*), a pair of wooden sandals, a jug or ewer, and an umbrella.

The orthodox form of ordination is thus completed. The candidate becomes a fully ordained monk.

This ceremony of ordination is supplemented by the worship of the deities: Bhairava, Mahakala, Vasundhara etc. with rituals and other parapharnelia, introduced later perhaps by the Tantric Buddhist monks

The ordained monk observes the restrictions imposed on him for four days only, and then approaches his Guru again and tells him that he is unable to lead the life of a monk and requests him to relieve him of the *Pravrajyavrata* and the ten observances (*siksapadas*) and to permit him to take up the disciplinary practices of a Bodhisattva. The Guru readily assents to his request, admitting that it is difficult to observe the rules and restrictions of *Pravrajya-vrata*. Thereafter the ordained monk becomes a house-holder but he gains the privilege of acting as officiating priests or Gubhajus.

Gubhajus, Vajracaryas And Bhiksus

The Gubhajus are to take the training of officiating priests. They learn the method of the ignition of daily fire with melted butter (*homa*), which is generally carried along with a deity. If they neglect to perform *homas,* they along with their descendants are degraded to the rank of *Bhiksus* or junior priests, who can act only as assistants of Gubhajus in rituals and ceremonies.

The Gubhajus are usually learned men (Pandit) and wear the sacred cord like the *Brahmins.* If he cultivates his Knowledge of *homa* and devotes himself to further studies of religious texts, he is raised to the rank of Vajracarya-arhat-bhiksu-buddha.

After attaining the status of a Vajracarya, he enjoys the highest rank of a priest and becomes entitled to perform ceremonies in connection with birth, marriage and death.[21]

Dress of a Vajracarya and a Bhiksu

The Vajracaryas and the Bhiksus put on a special dress. A Vajracarya puts on his head a bishop's mitre (tall cap) and a copper crown richly embossed with two rows of escutcheon (coat of arms) on which are embossed the images of Buddha and Tara. On the top is a Vajra horizontally placed on an escutcheon. In his hands he carries a Vajra and a Bell; from his neck up to the girdle hangs a rosary. He wears a yellow (*kasaya*) costume, consisting of a tight jacket with a thick-set skirt in pleats up to the girdle.

His assistant, the Bhiksu has a similar costume but with a different insignia. He puts on a coloured cap and a piece of wrapping cloth joined by gilt buttons . His rosary is of the simple type hanging from his neck and he carries in his hands a stick (*khikkhari*) and a begging bowl (*pindapatra*).

Position of Buddhism

From the historical survey made above, it is apparent that Buddhist evangelists reached Nepal sometime before the Christian era but they could not impregnate the people with the spirit of Buddhism and the monastic system of life. They made a superficial impression on the Kiratas and Newars, the earliest inhabitants of

Nepal, by acquainting them with the bare moral precepts About the 7th/8th centuries A.D., the ruling dynasties became interested in the religion, made substantial donations for erecting stupas and monasteries, but both the rulers and the common people did not give up their earlier faith in Saivism. They found in both Hinduism and Buddhism some common features, and tried to place Siva and Buddha on the same level. The fact that the Newars gave preference to Buddhism shows that the Buddhist evangelists were partially successful in winning over community to their faith although they could not completely wean them from their animistic beliefs and Brahmanic rituals. The existence of ancient *stupas* indicates that Buddhism had many adherents in ancient Nepal.

The Newars, however, could not rise up to the ideal of orthodox monasticism and produce self-sacrificing monks to take up spiritual practices for the attainment of the goal. It is for this reason, they readily succumbed to the caste distinction on lines parallel to that of the Brahmanas. Their monks lost no time to give up their celibacy and get married and to become fathers of families. They imitated the life of the Brahmanic priests with a view to lead an easy-going life.

As a matter of fact, the monasteries became denuded of celibate monks and novices, and were filled up by householders engaged in secular business. In Kashmir also, there is an instance of a similar monastery built by Yukadevi, wife of King Meghavahana, who was a great patron of Buddhism. Yukadevi built a magnificent monastery in one half of which, she placed those Bhiksus whose conduct conformed to the precepts, and in the other half those who were married and had children, cattle and property. The latter were being looked down for their life as a householder (Rajatarangini, iii. 12). In the 17th century, a king of Kathmandu and Bhatgaon built 25 Viharas naming them as *Nairvanikas* meant exclusively for celibate monks. Thus, it seems that there were, in Nepal as also in Kashmir, kings and queens who desired for celibate monks and not married priests, although the latter could not be denied residence in monasteries.

The Newars, however, adhered primarily to the Buddhist faith and secondarily to Saiva. They worshipped first the Buddhas and Bodhisattvas and then the Brahmanic deities, Siva and Visnu, while the Hindus reveresed this sequence of worship. It seems that the Nepalese maintained a balance between the two religions e.g. there is a Svayambhu Purana along with a Pasupati Purana. There is also another Purana with the title Buddha Purana in which Buddha has been made an incarnation of Visnu. There were two magnificent temples, one of Svayambhunath dedicated to Adi Buddha and the other of Pasupatinath enshrining Siva. It may be observed in this connection, that the symbol of Svastika was adopted by both the religions, but the Buddhists made it right-handed while the Hindus left-handed. Both the cults prevailed in the country all along, the Buddhist cult among the common people while the Brahmanic cult among the ruling classes. In this connection the remarks of Hiuen Tsang may be quoted here. He writes that the Nepalese believed both in false and true religion. The Buddhist monasteries and Deva temples touched each other. There were above 2000 ecclesiastices who were attached to both vehicles. The kings of Nepal were Ksatriya Licchavis, and they were eminent scholars, believing in Buddhism.

In Nepal-mahatmya, appears the line (There the Buddha predominates) while in a Buddhist manuscript appear the following lines:-

(What you desire out of the favour of Buddha was through the grace of Pasupati.)

The Newars developed a language of their own. They became excellent scribes and calligraphists. Their script was a development of the Gupta script of the 5th/6th Century A.D. One of the important features of their culture was the love for cailigraphy and earnestness in copying the Buddhist manuscripts, which were taken to Nepal by the fugitive monks of Nalanda, Vikramasila and Odantapuri after the onslaught of the Moslems in Bihar.

Nepal came into a close contact with the monks of the three monasteries of Bihar in the 10th Century A.D. In these monasteries at that time, the study and practices of Tantrayana became predominant and so this form of Buddhism with its divinities was introduced in Nepal It was also allied to Tantric Saivism.

Taranatha, the Tibetan historian, furnishes us with the names and particulars of few monks who went to Nepal. They are:

(i) Vasubandhu, the famous author of the Abhidharmakosa, after sending this work of his to Sanghabhadra, went to Nepal on his way from Kashmir to Nalanda.

(ii) Vajradeva, a great poet, a layman, went to Nepal and composed a poem criticizing a heretical Yogini of Nepal, who cursed him with the disease of leprosy. For getting rid of the disease, he implored Avalokitesvara and composed in three months in Sragdhara metre 100 stotras, enlogising him. He then visualized him and got himself freed of leprosy. He *stotras* became famous all over India.

(iii) Vagisivarakirti of Varanasi was the western *dvarapandita* of Vikramasila. He was a sthavira of the Mahasanghika School. He mastered both the Sutras and the Tantras. In the second half of his life he went to Nepal with a large number of female disciples, for which his sanctity was doubted by the people of Nepal but the king of Santapuri erected a Cakrasambara temple and requested him to invite a Ganacakra to inaugurate the temple.

In Taranatha relates the advent of the Moslems and as a result of which, the monks of Vikramasila and Odantapuri went to the different parts of India, evidently with their manuscript treasures Two of them came to Nepal. They are:

(i) Buddhasri, the head of Vikramasila after Sakyasri, was a native of Nepal. He returned to his homeland and taught the Paramitayana and the secret Mantrayana. He observed the Tantric form of conduct.

(ii) Ratnaraksita of Vikramasila was vastly learned like Sakyasri but he specialized in Mantrayana, and thereby he acquired immense magical powers. He visualised Kalacakra, Cakrasarnbara, Yamari etc. Two years ahead he foresaw the advance of Moslems, and so with a great number of his disciple, he left Vikramasila and reached Kashmir and Nepal. He went also for a short time to Tibet, where he wrote a commentary on *Samvarodaya*.

The eastern mountainous region of Nepal, touching the border of Tibet was inhabited mostly by Lepchas and other tribes using

Tibetan dialects and having a close affinity to the Tibetans. They became the followers of the Bon-po religion and erected Bon-po temples, e.g in Chakra village, and inherited some Buddhist articles of faith. King Strongbtsan-sgam-po and his successors (9th Century) made inroads into Nepal, conquered and ruled over the northeastern region of Nepal. This Tibetan conquest, led to further extension of Mahayana and Tantrayana Buddhism in Nepal and introduced some Mahayana and Tantrayanic principles and divinities as a veneer on Saivism. These could, however, neither supersede Sivaism not superimpose Buddhism on Saiva religion and divinities.

Both from Bihar and Tibet the Buddhist evangelists, imbued with Tantricism, propagated the Tantric phase of Buddhism in Nepal, with its Mantras, Mandalas and other secret practices.

It is therefore not at all surprising that the form of Buddhism in Nepal was Mahayanic and Tantric, and the Nepalese worshipped their divinities, the Dhyani Buddhas, Bodhisattvas, goddess Tara in her different forms as also the Yoginis, placing Sakyamuni in the background Prof. Levi paid a visit to a Vihara, Tyekam-bahal, where he noticed in the chapel an image of Sakyamuni flanked by the images of Lokesvara and Maitreya. On the top of the image there was a superb wood-panel depicting Mahavairocana, having in his hands a rosary, a sword, a club and a book. There were in the courtyard images of Amoghasiddhi, Aksoobya, Ratnasambhava and Padmapani. He came across a copy of Sakyamuni-stotra composed by Indra with a local commentary.

In the Buddha Purana, there is a fantastic account of the life of Sakyamuni. The Nepalese adore the footmarks of Sakyamuni Buddha. In the footmarks, there are carving or painting of the auspicious signs, viz. *Srivatsa, Padma, Dhvaja, Kalasa, Chattra, Matsya, Sankha* and *Cakra* [curl of hair on the breast, lotus, flag, jar, umbrella, whisk or fly-flap fish, conch-shell and concentric circles). These auspicious signs are more Brhamanic than Buddhistic. Hence, it is apparent that worship of Sakyamuni did not form an integral part of Nepalese Buddhism

The chief Buddhist divinity was Adi Buddha and the emanations out of Him.

Stupas

There are five ancient Caityas attributed to Emperor Asoka. These are on the model of the stupas at Sanchi and Taxila, but these do not enshrine any relics. The five Caityas are in Patan, a suburb of Kathmandu on its south-east. Of these, one Caitya is in the centre of the town and four in the four corners around the town. Caityas are just hemispherical mounds of bricks on a brick platform. Against the sides of the Caitya there are inset vaults enshrining in each of them one of the four Buddhas.

There are several stupas of this type of a late date scattered over Kathmandu and its neighbourhood.

Usually at the top of a stupa, there is a chapel dedicated to Vairocana. On its four sides there are also chapels in the innermost recesses, containing images of the four Dhyani-Buddhas, viz. Amitabba, (or Padmapani) Ratna-sambhava, Aksobhya and Amoghasiddhi.[29]

The glory of Nepalese Buddhism, is the Caitya of Svayambhunath standing on a 400 ft. high hillock on the western end of Kathmandu The Caitya is of immense dimension and proportion. Its style of architecture is the same as that of the ancient stupas. Its decorative features, however, are Lamaistic. On each of its tour sides are painted wide open eyes in red, white and black colour. On its eastern side at the end of the stairs is placed a gilt Vajra locally called Dorje guarded by two lions of stone placed on a stone disc called Vajradhatu-mandala. An oil lamp is always kept burning there.

The name Svayambhu is derived according to the tradition given in the Svayambhu Purana from Adi Buddha who manifested himself at the spot in the form of a flame of fire regarded as self-existent eternal and undecaying.

The credit of creating a temple for its preservation is given to Manjusri Bodhisattva. Adi Buddha is self-born and so the Nepalese worship him as Svayambhu. He is always in Nirvana and is issued out of Sunyata. Through his meditation appeared the five Dhyani Buddhas representing Pravrtti (manifestation), viz. Vairocana, Aksobhya, Ratnasambhava, Amitabha and Amoghasiddhi, Symbolising the five elements (Skandhas) viz, Rupa, Vedana,

Samjna, Sanskara and Vijnana. They in turn by their knowledge and contemplation brought into being five Dhyani Bodhisattvas, viz. Samantabhadra, Vajrapani, Ratnapani, Avalokitesvara of Padmapani and Visvapani respectively. The Bodhisattvas are believed to be creators of the Changing Universe. The present world is a creation of Avalokitesvara, who is protected by Buddha Amitabha. As his instructor appeared the human Buddha, Sakyamuni.

The appearance of Avalokitesvara out of Svaymbhu or existent, the Adi Buddha (the Primordial Buddha), also called Adinatha, is related in the later metrical version of the *Karandavyuha*. In *Mahayane-Sutralankara* Asanga denies the possibility of the conception of one beginingless (anaditah) Buddha or several Buddhas on account of the Mahayanic conception of Dharmakaya. Hence he comments saying "na can kascid adi-buddho'sti vina sambhareṅa". On the basis of this comment of Asanga, Prof. Winternitz (A History of India Literature, II, p. 306) inferred that Asanga referred to the Tantric conception of Adibuddha. The conception of Avalokitesvara, as found in the *Karandayuha* may be regarded as prior to that of Adibuddha. As a matter of fact the conception of Adibuddha was given currency in the *Kalacakratantra* at a much later date i.e. about the 10th Century.

According to the Svayambhu-purana, the Caitya of Svayambhunath of Kathmandu was erected first by Pracandadeva, king of Gauda, who abdicated his throne to enter into the order of monks and was given the religious name of Santikara-bhiksu. This however lacks corroboration by any inscription. The Caitya was repaired by Sivadeva Malla in 1593 and since then it was maintained by the Tibetans. About a century later, a Lama of Lhasa fixed gilt copper plates to the bell-tower and put up a gilt parasol. Lama Karmapa came to Nepal to bless the king and the people in 1751, when he took up the repair work of the Caitya and spent a large amount of gold and copper for 7 years for completing the work of renovation. Thereafter, for over a century, repairs and addition were made and these altered the original structure by putting up in chaotic order caityas, steles, images of Dhyani Buddhas and images of Vajrayana deities, colossal images of Buddha in black, white or red colour. These haphazard additions spoiled the grandeur of the Caitya. There are even steles on which is inscribed a *stotra* recounting the history of the Mallas, from pratapamalla, and another containing a bilingual inscription in Sanskrit and Tibetan of the 18th century.

Budhnath

The stupa of Budhnath is the second Buddhist stupa, next in importance to Svayambhunath. It stands on the river Bagmati between Gokarna and the temple of Pasupatinath. The Caitya is an edifice of unusual proportions, consisting of three symmetrical parts, the base, the hemisphere and the crown.

There are two traditions about its erection. One is that King Manadeva who committed parricide involuntarily prayed to Vajrayogini, the Trantric goddess of Vajrayoga for expiation of his sin. He was directed by the goddess to build the sanctuary of Budhnath, which he did in due course. He composed also stotra., very popular in Nepal eulogising the Triratna.

The other tradition current in Tibet is given by Waddell in his Lamaism. According to this tradition, a girl of pig-herd's family of Magute village in Nepal after marriage had four sons. She took up the profession of herding and rearing geese for the wealthy. She amassed much wealth and begged of the king of Nepal for a piece of land. She with her four sons, a servant, an ass and an elephant collected earth and bricks and started the construction of the Stupa. She died four years after commencing the work and her sons carried on the construction and completed it in due course. After completion, the sons received miraculously from heaven the relics of Tathagata Kasyapa and enshrined them in the Stupa. This stupa is worshipped by the Newars and Murmis as also by the Tibetan pilgrims.

Apart from these two magnificent stupas, there are hundreds of small stupas in the towns and villages of Nepal. There are clusters of stupas and temples in the cities of Kathmandu, Patan and bhatgaon. The existence of these stupas and temples in Nepal from the ancient times proves beyond doubt that Buddhism had a firm footing there in the ancient and medieval periods of Nepalese history. The religion lost its hold upon the people after the reign of Thakuris and Gurkhas who revived Brahmanism. The Gurkhas, however, at first, divided their patronage between Hinduism and

Buddhism. In a temple of Tundi Khal, the Gurkhas worshipped the deity as Mahakala while the Buddhists worshipped the same deity as Padmapani. The image, how ever, has in its tiara the figure of Amitabha. The Gurkhas allowed the Tibetan pilgrims freely to worship Svayambhunath and Budhnath. In both these stupas appears the mantra "Om Mani Padma Hum". The revival of Brahmanism led to the degeneration of Buddhist monks, who became house-holders, engaging themselves in different vocations, leaving the superficial maintenance of the religious beliefs to the Newars of higher castes, the Vajracaryas and Bhiksus, who also led a family life and converted the monasteries into dwellings of families of the priesthood.

The Buddhist divinities worshipped in various temples are Manjusri, Avalokitesvara including his manifestation as Matsyendranath Aksobhya, Amoghasiddhi, the Yoginis and the Taras in different colours. Sakyamuni Buddha is also worshipped in some temples but more importance is given to the worship of Manjusri and Avalokitesvara. In Nepal, Manjusri has in some cases been treated as a female deity while the Hindus looked upon it as Sarasvati, the goddess of learning Much may be written on these divinities, but at present this account has been left out. In his Indian Buddhist Iconagraphy, Dr. B. Bhattacharyya has described in detail the images of many of these divinities of Nepal.

5
The Nepal Mandala

The historians of Nepal have given different views about the origin of Nepal. Some historians have argued that the country was named Nepal as a sage called 'Ne' had protected it. Some argued on the basis of *Swayambhu Purana*, that the country was called Nepal Mandala because it was ruled judiciously by Dharmakar, the first king of Nepal. Nepal grammarians of Nepal Bhasha are of the view that Nepal is also called *Nepa*.

According to ancient Buddhist text, *Mulasarvasti vadavinaya*, *Shakyas* of Kabilvastu (Kapilvastu) and Baniyas of Sravasti, came to *Newal* (Nepal) from the north Sometime later, Bhikshu Ananda also entered Newal. The word *Kabilvastu* refers to Kapilvastu and *Newal* refers to Nepal. It is to be recalled that the indigenous people of Nepal call themselves *Nepami or Newami.* Other people call them *Newar.*

Another Buddhist text *Manjushrimula Kalpa* has mentioned Manadeva as king of Nepal Mandala. Researchers have guessed that the time of the composition of Mulasarvastivadavinaya is 2 century A.D. And the time of the composition of Manjushriulakalpa is not beyond the reign of Manadeva (464-506 A.D). *Swayambhu* Purana, the Buddhist Purana text, has mentioned Nepal Mandala. The word Nepal Mandala has also been carved in a Licchavi inscription.

Vajracharyas often use the word Nepal Mandala. In each and every Buddhist worship activity, first of all Nepal Mandala is uttered and only after this, Kantipur, Latitpur and Bhaktapur are mentioned. It is thus evident that the use of Nepal Mandala is prevalent since the pauranic time to the present day. Contexwise Nepal Mandala may mean different things. An attempt is made here to explain about Nepal Mandala. The Buddhism of Nepal was greatly influenced by the Tibetan Buddhist tradition. The Buddhism of the Kathmandu Valley was influenced by Theravada Buddhism imported from Myanramar (Burma), Sri Lanka, Thailand, etc. since the last five decades. After from these two traditions, Buddhism prevailing in Nepal since the ancient times to the present day with its own typical tradition, culture, rituals, art is the original Buddhism of Nepal.

Nepal lipi (script of Nepal) Nepal Samvat, Nepal Bhasha have helped preserve the originality and identity of Nepal. Buddhism obtaining in Nepal and the traditional culture has also done the same. The terms like Nepal Mandala, Nepal Samvat. Nepal Bhasha, the religion, art and culture of Nepal are all connected with the Buddhism of Nepal and its tradition.

According to the Buddhist tradition of Nepal, Vajracharya Gurus, Shakya used to practise Samadhiyoga in 24 important religious sites of the Kingdom of Nepal. This is called *purva-seva* or *pitha-seva*. This tradition is alive to the present time. These pithas are the following:

1	Chandralakhu	-	Pritha inside Narayanhitti Royal Palace
2	Pasikwo	-	East of Tindhara Pathshala and behind Royal Nepal Academy.
3	Kamaladi	-	Kamaladi Ganeshsthan pitha
4	Lumadhi	-	Bhadrakalipitha near Tundikhel
5	Phiwo	-	Pitha near Army Headquarters
6	Pachali Naiajima	-	Pachalibhairav Pitha
7	Kanga	-	Kangesvaripitha. The way from Maruhiti and Dhoka Tole
8	Luti	-	Indrayanipitha, near Shovabhagavati
9	Tanaju	-	Phaikha, Harisidhi behind, Swayambhu
10	Mhasapi	-	Mhepi, Nayabazar
11	Todana	-	Nara, Tunaldevi
12	Kati	-	Danchhi, below Changu hill
13	Misido	-	Mahankali of Bhaktapur
14	Soruthi	-	Shankhamol, Patan
15	Jallandhar	-	Panga, Charkhala, charghar
16	Balkhu	-	Way to Machhenarayan

17	Gwakhu	-	Bhinduga, Chhetrapati, on the bank of river, on the border between Kathmandu and Dhading
8	Gadebheru	-	Devighat, Trisuli
19	Tupya	-	Navalinga (Bhadrakali), left of the way to Buddhanilkantha
20	Sadukuna	-	Sadukola Sankhu
21	Sameda	-	Dolalghat
22	Otirtha	-	Koshi area, Dumjaghat
23	Tyanga	-	Bade Tyanga, Tikabhairab
24	Jhanga	-	Jhangu, Koduwal

The above 24 places have been classified into three chakras (circles). The first eight pithas (1-8) have been included into the first circle. The second eight (9-16) pithas have been included into the second circle. The final eight (17-24) pithas have been included into the third circle. Kantewar Chhetrapala at Indrachowk is considered to be the centre of all the three circles.

The first circle is called *chitta* (consciousness) chakra. The second one is called *vaka* (speech) chakra. And the third one is called *kaya* (action) *chakra*. All the three chakras are also called chitaamandala, Vakamandala and Kayamandala respectively.

Picture No. 1 : Nepal Mandala

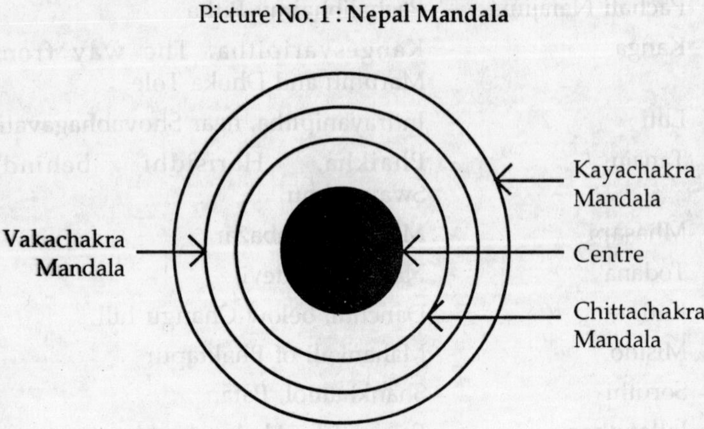

If we look at all the 24 pithas or Chinttachakra, Vakachakra and Kayachakra as an organized unit, we have the picture of great mandala. This is the main reason why Nepal is called Mandala. The final circle represents the climax of Nepal Mandala. The final circle is also the boundary of Vajrayana Buddhism in Nepal. Now let me discuss how Nepal was conceived as a mandala and kayachakra.

Vajrayana is an important branch of Buddhism. It is not necessary to tell about the popularity of Vajrayana and its influence and spread. Mandala occupies an important place in Vajrayana. The teaching of Vajrayana is not complete without Mandala. Without it the teaching of Vajrayana is not authentic. It is difficult to mention the number of Mandalas required in Vajrayana education. This is to say that there are innumerable Mandalas in Vajrayana. One of them is chakramandala, a short account of which is given below.

Picture No. 2 : **Nepal Mandala**

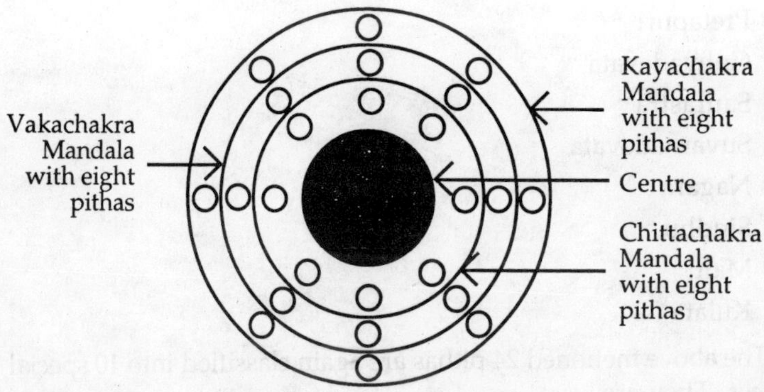

According to Chakrasamvara mandala, 24 cells in Chittacakra Vakchakra and Kayachakra mandalas are known by the following names:

Chittachakra:

1. Pullilamalaya
2. Jallandhar
3. Odiyana

4. Aburda
5. Godavari
6. Rameshwari
7. Devikot
8. Malawa

Vakachakra:

9. Kamarupa
10. Odra
11. Trisakuni
12. Koshala
13. Kalinga
14. Lanpaka
15. Kanchhi
16. Himalaya

Kayachakra:

17. Pretapuri
18. Guhyadevata
19. Saurastra
20. Suvarnadevata
21. Nagara
22. Sindhu
23. Malu
24. Kulata

The above metioned 24 pithas are again classified into 10 special places. They are:

- Pullilamalaya Jallandhar, Odiyana and Aburda fall under pitha.
- Godavari, Rameswari, Devikot and Malawa fall under sub-pitha.
- Kamarupa and Odra fall under Trisakuni and Koshala sub-area.
- Kalinga and Lanpak fall under *chhandoha* and Kanchhi and Himalaya fall under *sub-chhandoha*.

- Pretapuri and Guhyadevata fall under *Melapaka*. And Saurastra and Suvarnadwipa fall under *sub-chhandoha*.
- Nagara and Sindhu fall under *Samshan* and Malu and Kulata fall under *sub-Sanshan*.

Picture No. 3 : **Nepal Mandala**

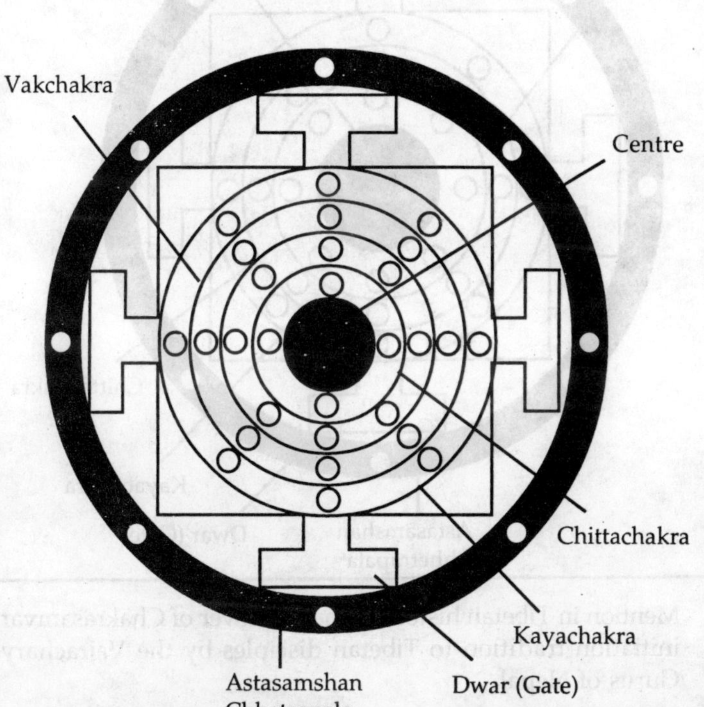

The center, the three circles and 24 cells of Nepal Mandala and Chakrasamvara Mandala are identical. Therefore, Nepal Mandala was conceived on the basis of Chakrasamvara Mandala. Nepal Mandala may be called a realization of Chakrasamvara Mandala.

There are other possible reasons.

a. Chakrasamvara is the principal deity of Vajrayana.
b. Compulsory chakrasamvara initiation of Vajracharyas, Shakyas, Urayas in Nepal.

Picture No. 4 : **Nepal Mandala**

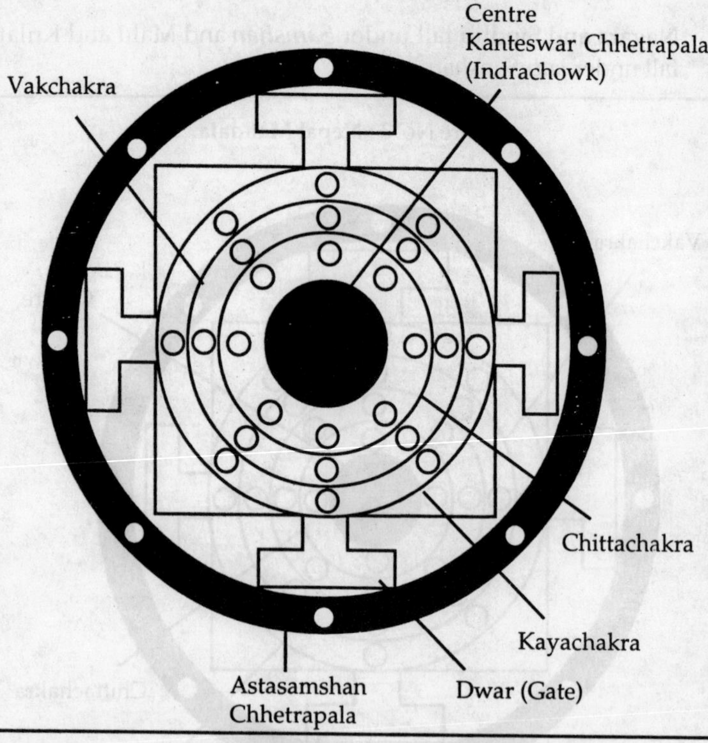

c. Mention in Tibetan history of the handover of Chakrasamvara initiation tradition to Tibetan disciples by the Vajracharya Gurus of Nepal.

d. Continuation of *Purva Seva* in accordance with Chakrasamvara tradition.

e. Only those who are initiated into Chakrasamvara are entitled to *Purva Seva*.

f. Deity in Agam houses in most of the vihars of Nepal is chakrasamvara.

g. Availability of tantras related to chakrasamvara in adequate number in Nepal.

h. *Tri samadhi* (three kinds of samadhi) *Kriya* (activities) are compulsory in Buddhist worship activities in Nepal.

Chakrasamvara mandala is not the only basis of Nepal Mandala. But it is only one of the factors connected with Vajrayana.

Just as there is the practice of *Purva Seva* on the basis of Chakrasamvara Mandala by conceiving Nepal Mandala, simplarly, there is the tradition of *purva seva* on the basis of *Swayambhu Purana* by conceiving Nepal as a different mandala. It is to be recalled here that when Manjudevacharya cut Kanpotalaparvat, water began to flow out of the valley. Even then the water did not dry up. Water was coming out from the root of lotus flower. In order to stop this Manjudevacharya did *Jalastambhanyoga*. On completion of this yoga water began to come out from the root of the lotus. At that time Manjudevacharya had a *darshan* (glimpse) of the origin as well as sight of *Sri Nairatmadevi* (Hevajranairatma) and other vajrayana deities in the water that flowed out. Here, Sri Nairatmadevi and other deities must mean Sri Hevajranairatma and Sri Hevajranairatma Mandala.

According to the account of Swayambhu Purana, the establishments of Hevajranairatma by Manjudevacharya and Shantipur by Shantikaracharya is known. It is a traditional belief that the presiding deity of Shantipur is Mahasamvara. It is but natural that Mahasamvara should be connected with Mahasamvara Mandala. It is very much likely that Nepal Mandala was conceived in the tradition of Mahasamvara Mandala.

As mentioned in Swayambhu Purana, Manjudevacharya initiated Dharmashri Mitra, the Acharya of Vikramshila Mahavihar by writing the mandala of Dharmadhatu Vagisvara. He also gave instructions of *Dwadasachchyar*. Then Swayambhu chaitya became famous by the name of *Dharmadhatu Vagisvara*, Dharmadhatu Mandala is the foundation of Dharmadhatu Vagisvara Chaitya.

Within the Nepal Mandala itself, Lalitpur Mandala, Bhaktapur Manda and Madhyapur Mandala have been conceived. Vajracharya and Shakyas are used to visiting the separate eight pithas of Lalitpur. There is also Kirtipur Chakramandala.

Vajracharyas who are involved in Bodhisattva charya activities create at least one chakra wherever they settle and construct the vihar there for propagation of Buddhism.

Eight pithas in Lalitpur Mandala,15 Bhaktapur Mandal,16 and Madhyapur Mandala 17 are as follows:

Lalitpur Mandala:

1. Nakhupitha
2. Balkumari
3. Yeppa
4. One on the way to Chovar
5. Dhantil
6. One on the way to Jawalakhel
7. Sikubi
8. Mahalakshmi

Bhaktapur Mandal

1. Centre at Bhairab – Tamadhitol
2. Brahmayani
3. Maheswari
4. Kaumari
5. Vaishnavi
6. Indrayani
7. Chamundra
8. Mahalakshmi

Madhyapur Mandal - Thimi

1. Brahmayani
2. Maheswari
3. Kaumari
4. Vaisnavi
5. Indrayani
6. Barahi
7. Chamundra
8. Mahalakshmi

Now, an attempt is made to present Nepal Mandala from the angle of Prithvimandala.

According to the Buddhist tradition, there are four continents and four sub-continents. The names of continents are:

1. Purva videhadwipa - in the east
2. Jambudwipa - in the south
3. Apargodavari - in the west
4. Uttara kuru - in the north

The names of four sub-continents are

1. Yaudwipa - in the Agnaya side.
2. Randwipa - in the Nairitya side.
3. Laudwipa - in the Vayuvya side.
4. Waudwipa - in the Ishan side.

Among the above four continents, Jambudwipa is a very important one. According, to the Buddhist tradition Jambudwipa is divided into ten pithas. If study is done on the initiation of Vajracharyas, the role of Nepal Mandala in the Buddhism of Nepal becomes clear.

6

Nepal's Buddhist Traditions

Buddhism & Its Teachings

Lord Buddha appeared in this world with the sole purpose of benefitting all sentient beings of the Triple Realm. His appearance in this world is a very rare phenomenon and is the outcome of the collective merits of his disciples and the beings that are to be trained under him. Out of great compassion Buddha Shakyamuni revealed many different means to attain enlightenment and to win liberation from the cycle of birth and death. Buddha Shakyamuni set forth Three Wheels of Law to suit varying degrees of intelligence and receptivity.

At a place called Mrigadavana (Deer Park) near Varanasi, Shakyamuni Buddha turned the First wheel of Law which constituted the doctrines of the Four Noble Truths and Eight-fold Path and it is designated as Shravakayana.

At a place called Gridha-kuta hill (Vulture Peak) near Rajgir, the Buddha turned the Second Wheel of Law which constituted the doctrines of Emptiness and Selflessness of the person and phenomena. These doctrines are vividly preserved in Prajnaparamita literature and Vaipulya sutras. This approach was later known as Mahayana or Path of the Bodhisattva.

At Vaisali, on the other hand, the Buddha turned the Third Wheel of Law which constituted the doctrines of Buddha-nature as described in Tathagatagarbhasutra Mahaparinirvanasutra and Dharanisvararaja sutra.

At various places such as Dhanyakataka, Sriparvat, Kamakhya, Sirihatta, Purnagiri, Odiyana etc. the Buddha revealed the path of Mantra to his highly gifted disciples as a shorter path to attain enlightenment. This approach was termed as Vajrayana, which integrates all three vehicles.

Essence of Sutra Tradition

Refuge: We live in an ocean of samsara whose depth and extent cannot be measured. We are troubled again and again by afflictions of lust and hatred. To what refuge should we go then? In our childhood when we are in trouble we seek the refuge of our parents. But our parents are themselves suffering and are the victims of lust, hatred and delusion. They cannot be the source of refuge. A source of refuge must completely overcome all the defects forever i.e. it must be free of all faults. Only the Buddha has extinguished all faults and gained all the qualities and attainments.

Thus we take refuge in the Buddha. Since Dharma is the unmistaken path leading to enlightenment, we take refuge in Dharma which eliminates all our causes of suffering. We take refuge in Sangha who supports and guides our dharma practice. All Buddha images are representatives of the Buddha, Scriptures are the representatives of Dharma, Bhikshus and Bodhisattvas are the representatives of Sangha. Taking refuge in Buddha, Dharma and Sangha is termed as outer refuge.

The objects of inner refuge are Gurus, Istadevas and Dakinis. They will he described in a more elaborative way in subsequent chapters. And the secret refuge according to Vajrayana tradition is to realize Dharmakaya, Sambhogakaya and Nirmanakaya.

Karma & Its Effect

The main teachings of the Buddha constitute the Law of Cause and Effect. Although all the beings in samsara seek joy and shun sufferings they are ignorant of the cause of happiness or sorrow. In fact, the happiness and suffering of the sentient beings are the results of their own virtuous or non-virtuous actions.

Guru Suvarnadvipa of Indonesia once told Atisha Dipamkara, "Until you attain freedom from the delusion of ego-grasping, follow the Law of Cause and Effect."

With the purpose of creating fear in the minds of people from indulging in non-virtuous acts and understanding the essence of defilements, various wrathful images are being manifested by the enlightened beings specifically in Vajrayana tradition.

Tathagatagarbha (Buddha-Nature)

All sentient beings possess Buddha-nature which means primordial wakefulness free from thought constructs present in the mind. By virtue of possessing Buddha-nature, one is able to become an enlightened one. But in order to realize Buddha-nature, the precious human body is needed. The precious human body enables the accumulation of merits and wisdom, which are needed for the realization of the enlightenment.

Because of this Buddha-nature of our mind an enormous pantheon of Vajrayana deities is being manifested in order to tame sentient beings and assist the practitioners in eliminating their obstructions to enlightenment. In Tantric Buddhist tradition we visualize Buddhas, Yidams, Dakinis and Bodhisattvas as enlightened states to be attained. The practice of deity yoga is compatible only because we have Buddha-nature.

Impermanence

The Buddha says that all composite things are impermanent. They are liable to disintegrate or are perishable in nature. The realization of impermanence is extremely important in all level of spiritual development including Bodhisattva levels. Instruction on impermanence is imperative as a remedy to eliminate attachment to sensuous experience of this life, which is the essential condition for the attainment of Buddhahood.

In most of the Dharmapala imagery the bone ornaments are the symbols of the impermanent nature of phenomena. The wrathful appearances of Yidam or Dharmapala deities are also the embodiments of impermanence. When we realize the impermanent nature of our body and phenomena we are terrified. Then slowly we understand that we all have to die, leaving behind everything except virtuous and non-virtuous deeds done in our life time.

Suffering of Samsara

The Buddha's main concern in teaching the Four Noble Truths is relinquishing of sufferings of the samsara. The entire Sutra literature and its commentaries deal with suffering of samsara and ways or means to eliminate the sufferings. The practice of Four

Noble Truths enables one to the path of liberation. Upon realizing the vicious state of samsara, one turns one's own mind away from pleasure of this world and thus approaches liberation, relinquishing all the causes of suffering (as in the Theravada tradition).

In the Mahayana tradition, the practitioners (Bodhisattvas) although undergoing all the sensual experiences of the world, do not do so for themselves but for the sake of others. And through such activities they accumulate merits and wisdom and attain buddhahood in the future.

Similarly in the Vajrayana tradition, such motives as described above are being depicted in various forms of imagery.

Bodhicitta

The foundation of Mahayana tradition lies in the practice of Bodhicitta. The text Abhisamayalamkara states:

"The formation of an enlightened attitude (Bodhicitta) is the desire for enlightenment for the benefit of others".

For the attainment of enlightenment, Bodhicitta is essential at all bodhisattva levels. There is no Buddha or Bodhisattva who lacked it. So all the Highest Yoga Tantra deities who are depicted in sexual union with their consorts are, however, the embodiment of the union of Bodhicitta (male) and wisdom (female). It is said that enlightenment is impossible without these two aspects.

Essence of Vajrayana Tradition

The secret Mantrayana is hidden (*skt. Guhya*) because it is not appropriate for the common people. It is however, fit for the advanced practitioner well versed in Emptiness, Bodhicitta and Renunciation. There are two factors in the Mantra vehicle:

a) Pride in oneself as the deity

b) Vivid appearance of that deity

Divine pride protects one from ordinary appearance and through this change in attitude the pride of being a deity emerges. Forms are viewed as the emanation of the deity and the deity itself is the product of the mind and sounds as the mantras of that deity.

In order to embark on this practice of Vajrayana one should have the initiation or empowerment of a particular deity from a qualified Guru. By this empowerment the disciple will learn the exact nature and classification of the tantric system into which he is to be introduced. He will also know the nature of mandala and prerequisites for the disciple and the stage of the empowerment to be followed. It is desirable for the artists and sculptors to have at least one initiation of Highest Yoga Tantra under a qualified Guru and learn fundamental tenets of Mahayana and Vajrayana practices.

Sacred Pledge (*skt. Samaya*)

Keeping vows, receiving the Initiation and the sacred word of honour are the foundation for the meditation on two stages of the tantric path. When one has received an abhiseka one should not forsake the complete set of 18 bodhisattva and 14 tantric vows. Breaking any of the root tantric vows would cause one to lose the effective power of the Initiation.

Developing & Completion Stage

In order to have the attainment of Buddhahood one must practice developing the first stage and only then should go on to practice completion stage. Through practicing 'developing stage' only, one may necessarily acquire the five fold miraculous power, yet, the practice of the 'developing stage' is the integral part of the path for attaining the highest goal i.e. Buddhahood. Generally 'developing stage' is the visualization of the meditational deity and his circle of mandala visualized clearly and simultaneously in all details. Here the artists must be careful in creating the images of various deities with due attention, following the cannonical texts or the instructions of a qualified tantric Buddhist master.

In profound 'completion stage' is the practice of meditation on emptiness on the nature of these deities. So proper care must be taken into consideration to produce images of a genuine nature so that it becomes the object of faith and devotion.

LEADING TENETS

Trikaya Doctrine

Dharmakaya

According to Mahayana Buddhist tradition, an enlightened being is said to possess two bodies: Truth Body and Form Body. It is said that through the practice of six perfections one accumulates merits and wisdom through which one realizes Dharmakaya as the result.

Dharmakaya is the stage of the mind free from dual obscuration i.e. obscuration to liberation and omniscience. The obscuration to liberation i.e. afflictive emotions (*skt. Kleshavarana*) pertains to the attitude of self grasping (*skt. Atmagrahadrsti*) and resulting defilement. Whereas obstruction to omniscience pertains to all preconceived ideas about the reality (*skt. Fneyasarana*). When one is free from all these constructive thought patterns, one spontaneously experiences the Dharmata of all knowable things. The knowledge of experiences of Dharmata of all phenomena is termed as Dharmakaya.

This stage of experience is called by different names such as Tathata, Emptiness and Yathabhuta. The Buddha says that one who sees this Dharmakaya sees the Buddha. The attainment of Buddhahood is just the realization of this Dharmakaya. According to Vajrayana tradition, this wisdom of Dharmakaya is classified into five wisdoms i.e. all pervasive wisdom, mirror-like wisdom, wisdom of equality, discriminative wisdom and all-accomplishing wisdom. This five forms of wisdom is represented by five transcendental Buddhas called Vairocana, Akshobhya, Ratna Sambhava, Amitabha and Amogha Siddhi. These five Buddhas are the source of vast pantheon of Vajrayana Buddhism. So all the deities both male and female are associated with these five Buddhas as their source of origin.

Dharmakaya, on the other hand, is said to be that stage when one purifies death, intermediate state and rebirth. When a practitioner dies they experiences the dissolution of four elements one after another. Their sense faculties do not function and only their consciousness supported by vital air become apparent and they experience Clear light of Death. If the deceased can experience and recognize this Clear light it is the same as realizing

Dharmakaya. Most of the Mahasiddhas who could not realize Dharmakaya in their life time, can realize it after death. It is said that in this stage of mind if one realizes clear knowing aspect and the empty nature of the mind it is called Dharmakaya. This two in one nature of mind is primordially present in every sentient being. Our own consciousness is in reality empty and cognizant, blissful and shining. The unity of them is the Dharmakaya state of Perfect Enlightenment.

Sambhogakaya

When one realizes Dharmakaya he is endowed with the wisdom of knowing nature as it is (*skt. Yathabhuta*) and with the wisdom of all existing objects of knowledge. Owing to the removal of all the veils and obstructions covering the mind his omniscient mind gives rise to twofold body i.e. Sambhogakaya and Nirmanakaya.

There are four characteristic features of Sambhogakaya Buddha. Firstly, he is always endowed with 32 major marks and 8o minor marks. Secondly, he always teaches Mahayana among the families of irreversible bodhisattvas. Thirdly, he resides in one specific buddha field. Fourthly, he perfectly enjoys that Buddha realm with great peace and happiness.

Sambhogakaya means 'perfect enjoyment body'. The bodhisattva since the beginning of his career has taken vows of relieving suffering of all sentient being and giving them peace and happiness. So he guides suffering beings to Bodhisattva level. The enjoyment body of Buddha then converts beginner bodhisattvas to perfect Enlightenment through guidance.

Hence, Sambhogakaya is very pure and perceptible only to realized Bodhisattvas. Enjoyment here means the fulfillment of his vows and aspirations of the Buddha. In Sambhogakaya there is no limit of capacity or ability of his body, speech and mind. Whatever he wishes or aspires for the qualities of the Buddha, he will get the fruit as he desires when he attains Buddhahood. For example Bhikshu Dharmakar, when he was a bodhisattva, made 48 vows and aspirations in order to relieve the suffering and to get himself established into Buddhahood. Later on according to his vows and aspirations, Bhikshu Dharmakar became Buddha Amitabha in Sukhavati heaven.

According to Tantric Buddhist tradition, all Buddhas like Vajradhara, Vajrasattva and Yidam deities appear in the form of Sambhogakaya. They have all sorts of ornaments and garments signifying the qualities of enlightenment. The multi-arm, multi-face and multi-emblems they hold are the embodiments of the qualities of enlightenment.

Sambhogakaya has eight qualities of mastery.

1. He is endowed with the mastery of body, which can take any shape or form to tame sentient beings according to their need.
2. He is endowed with mastery of speech, which has 64 qualities and can turn the wheel of dharma for sentient beings as needed.
3. He is endowed with mastery of mind, which possesses non-conceptual compassion.
4. He is endowed with unimpeded miraculous powers.
5. He is endowed with mastery of desire being unstained even when presented with sensual pleasures of all kinds.
6. He is like a wish-fulfilling gem fulfilling the desires and hopes of beings.
7. He resides in the pure abode of Akanistha continuously as the dharma king over three realms.
8. He is endowed with realization of one taste between Nirvana and Samsara signifying his mastery of all pervasiveness.

Hence all Buddhas, Bodhisattvas of high rank, Istadevatas i.e. Yidam Herukas are depicted in their Sambhogakaya aspects. Their specific color, emblems, faces are the metaphorical ways of expressing the qualities of enlightenment. For example 16-armed Mahakala represents the deity indicating 16 types of emptiness he represents. Four-armed Mahakala represents his dominion over four Maras, the (four obstructions on the path of Enlightenment). Yamantaka, who kills the Lord of death, represents the deathlessness aspect of perfect enlightenment.

In another context Samhhogakaya is also said to be an illusory body, which a dying sentient being experiences in the intermediate state after death. He will see various peaceful and wrathful deities, which are the emanations of his own thought forms. In Tantric

Buddhist tradition this mental body in the intermediate state is utilized for realization of illusory body and then Mahamudra.

Nirmanakaya

We have already said that an enlightened being has two bodies: Samhhogakaya and Nirmanakays. Sambhogakaya Buddha usually resides only in a pure Buddha field. Nirmanakays Buddha assumes innumerable forms or transform bodies according to the circumstances and attitudes of the sentient being to he converted or tamed. It is said in Prajna Sutra that one who practices the perfection of wisdom attains the supreme enlightenment and emanates many transformed bodies to suit the varying degrees of intelligence in ten different directions to convert the stubborn beings in the path of the dharma. This emanation body is of many kinds.

One such Nirmanakaya is called Supreme Nirmanakaya. The supreme Nirmanakaya is the body of Buddha having 32 marks and 80 minor marks. He is born as a human being and performs 12 principal deeds of the Buddha such as birth, display of skill in arts, marriage, renunciation, austerities, attainment of the Buddhahood, turning the wheel of dharma and his final passing away, etc. During the Buddha's historic career innumerable beings were liberated through his skill in means of 12 principal deeds The Buddha like Dipamkara, seven Buddhas, etc. ate supreme Nirmanakaya.

Another form of Nirmanakaya is a Tulku like the Dalai Lama who takes rebirth for specific number of times to convert the beings in the path of enlightenment.

Most of Gurus and Mahasiddhas belong to this category. Yet another form of Nirmanakaya is Created Nirmanakya. The Buddha once created a beautiful celestial lady in order to tame a haughty and proud queen named Khema, the consort of king Bimbisara. Queen Khema found the lady much more charming than herself Suddenly she saw that the lady collapsed and died. The queen then realized the impermanent nature of our human body and beauty. Later on she became the foremost lady disciple of the Buddha.

For Nirmanakaya, the emanated body, it is not necessary to be a human body only but it can be in animal forms such as monkey, elephant, bird, etc. also.

Gurus

In Vajrayana Buddhism, Gurus are of paramount importance. In fact, it is due to Gurus starting from the time of the Buddha Shakyamuni right upto present time, that the entire lineages of dharma teachings are being preserved and practiced. In the Theravada tradition Shakyamuni Buddha is also called Shasta i.e. the Guru of all devas and men. But in the Vajrayana tradition, Gurus like Padmasambhava, Tilopa, Naropa, Marpa, Milarepa, Tsong Khapa, Virupa and many others are also considered to be the representatives of the enlightenment, which Buddha Shakyamuni realized. Later on in the Vajrayana tradition also, the images of the Gurus were used to visualize to actualize the mind of Buddha.

Some Gurus are also considered to be the emanated bodies i.e. reincarnated Nirmanakaya of some Buddhas and Bodhisattvas like Amitabha, Manjusree or Avalokiteshvara.

Buddhas

In Vajrayana tradition all the Buddhas are called Gurus. However especially five transcendental Buddhas (*skt. Pancabuddha*) who represent the essence of five primordial defilements such as lust, hatred, delusion, pride and jealousy are mainly dealt with here. When one realizes the essence of these five delusions one achieves 'five wisdom'. The essence of lust is symbolized by Buddha Amitabha and is known as discriminating wisdom. The essence of delusion (*skt. moha*) is symbolized by Buddha Vairocana and is known as all pervasive wisdom. The essence of anger is symbolized by Buddha Akshobhya and is called Mirror-like wisdom. The essence of pride is symbolized by Buddha Ratna Sambhava and is known as Wisdom of Equality. The essence of Jealousy is symbolized by Buddha Amoghsiddhi and is known as all accomplishing wisdom. Thus primordial purity of these five defilements, which obscure our mind is represented by Pancabuddha.

These five Buddhas are not the subdivision of Buddha Shakyamuni nor do they have consorts and children of their own as some Buddhist scholars understand. These forms of Pancabuddha are in fact the metaphorical ways of expression of non-dual wisdom and skill in means. As previously mentioned they are Sambhogakaya Buddhas and can perform ceaseless activity for the benefit of all sentient beings.

Bodhisattvas

In the Mahayana Buddhist tradition Bodhisattvas are said to be of two kinds. One is Adi-karmika Bodhisattva who is a beginner, who has not realized perfect enlightenment and is still a learner. Firstly he or she develops enlightenment thought for the benefit of sentient beings and wishes for perfect enlightenment. Secondly there is a Bodhisattva who realizes emptiness face to face and attains the first Bodhisattva level. He gradually progresses till the tenth Bodhisattva level through the practice of the six perfections and Mahamudra.

Some of them even after attaining the level of Buddhahood, emanate forms and act like Bodhisattvas. As, for example, Buddhas like Avalokiteshvara, Manjusree, Vajrapani and some other high-ranking Bodhisattvas emanate numerous forms to tame the sentient beings in the manner of beginner Bodhisattvas. Shakyamuni Buddha himself took three incalculable aeons to complete his career as a Bodhisattva. Those who have attained the first level up to the tenth level of Bodhisattva have enormous power to benefit others.

Eight high ranking bodhisattvas who are no less than Shakyamuni Buddha himself in wisdom, compassion and powers, will be dealt with in the subsequent chapters. It is to be noted that Bodhisattvas can be a male or a female. All female divinities of genre Tara and protrectress deities are Bodhisattvas who work for the benefit of sentient beings as male counterparts do.

Istadevata (Yidam Deities)

In the Vajrayana Buddhist tradition Istadevata (Yidam) are called mind bound deities. Because the nature of these deities is the same as the nature of mind. The practitioners in Vajrayana Buddhism visualize Istadevatas such as Hevajra, Cakrasamvara, Kalacakra and others during developing stages of meditation (*skt. Utpattikrama*) as their Samatha and Vipasyana practice. They are originated from their seed syllables, which appear from a non-dual state of mind, free of thought constructs or state of emptiness. They are not mere imaginations. They are the visualized forms of enlightened minds. They are all Sambhogakaya Buddha forms emanated from a true mind. These deities have however, no real existence as such. But they are the emanated forms of enlightened mind.

Practitioners who have an affinity to these deities in one form or the other can develop their realization very quickly with these practices since these deities represent emotional inclination of the practitioners. If some practitioners like to have Avalokiteshvara, the other may opt for Arya Tara. Some practitioners of aggressive nature rather prefer wrathful deities to meditate or to identified with. In all the Tantric Buddhist tradition these deities are visualized clearly with different colors, forms, faces, hands, all with different ornaments.

The purpose of this deity yoga is to take the form of the deity and actualize his Buddha activities during meditation. This creative visualization method is used to achieve a form body endowed with 32 major marks and 80 minor marks i.e. Sambhogakaya. It is said that the fruit of Buddhahood must be achieved through a method, which has the form of the Buddha.

One of the characteristic features of the Yidam deity is the sexual imagery found in highest yoga tantra (Anuttara tantra). Upon confrontation with father-mother union (Yabyum) aspect of the Buddha, a casual observer may find it difficult and astonishing to understand the fearsome and erotic nature of the images in the context of Vajrayana Buddhism.

In Nepal this Tantric knowledge is said to he guarded by Nepalese Vajracharyas and in Tibet, by Tibetan Gurus. These Highest Yoga tantra deities are kept strictly secret and are to be seen by the initiated only. However such deities, which were kept secret in past, are now finding their way into the open for different reasons and consequently, the meanings or implication relating to these deities have been the subject of growing curiosity.

It is true that Vajrayana is the vehicle of 'skill in means', which utilizes even desire or lust to attain Buddhahood. Vajrayana being the path of transformation utilizes even sexual bliss to realize emptiness or nature of mind.

It is said that these practices of Highest Yoga tantra deities involving sexual imagery are appropriate for the most gifted practitioners only. Through such creative visualization process they develop experiences of emptiness of the highest standard, that is, Buddha-nature.

The examples of such tantras are Guhyasamaja, Hevajra, Kalacakra, etc. The Highest Yoga tantra claims that Buddhahood is possible within a single lifetime. Eighty-four mahasiddhas of India, Nepal and Tibet attained enlightenment in their own life time through the practice of such tantras.

Dakinis

In Tantric Buddhist tradition the practitioner takes refuge in the Triple Gem, which is referred to as the outer refuge. The objects of the inner refuge are said to be Gurus, Istadevas and Dakinis. Dakinis are obviously representatives of Sangha in the inner refuge. They are peaceful as well as wrathful. They wear bone ornaments. Some are in dancing posture. Some are even nude.

These Dakinis generally travel through empty space hence also called Sky-goers. They help the practitioners by eliminating different obstacles and by guiding to realization of the path to enlightenment. They are able to grant eight great powers (*skt. Astasiddhi*) to all devoted practitioners. Some Dakinis are animal faced like Simhavaktra (lion-faced), Vajravarahi (sow-faced), Sardulamukha (tiger-faced) and many others. Vajrayogini is said to be Sarva-Buddha Dakini who confers Buddhahood to the practitioners. These Buddha Dakinis are said to be the representatives of Wisdom or Prajnaparamita.

Dharmapalas (Protectors of Doctrine)

As the name suggests Dharmapalas are the divinities who help to protect the Buddha dharma from degeneration and they also act as defenders of the Buddha's doctrines. They are in general wrathful in appearance to terrify the sinners. In Nepal, Mahakala is considered to be the great wrathful Dharmapala whose image is installed inmost of the Buddhist viharas and temples.

Actually, all divinities of direction starting from Yamantaka are Dharmapalas. These protector deities are also called Lord of Knowledge (*skt. Vidyadhara*) indicating their status of high Bodhisattva level.

Dikpalas (The Deities of Direction)

Dikpalas or Lokapalas are the deities who correspond to the deities found in Hindu tantric tradition. All the eight mother goddesses starting from Camunda, Brahmayani, Kaumari, Indrayani, Varahi, etc. are considered as protectors of the dharma in Buddhist tradition, whereas in the Hindu tradition they are ultimate principle to be actualized.

In the Buddhist tradition the deities of direction include deities like Yama, Varuna, Indra, Vayu, Agni and others who have taken the oath to protect the practitioners and sasana of the Buddha's doctrines. In Gunakarandavyuha Sutra it is even said that Bodhisattva Avalokiteshvara emanated these Lokapalas to defend the Buddha sasana.

Vajrayana Buddhism incorporates almost all the Hindu deities as protectors of the dharma to eliminate obstacles on the path to enlightenment. The involvement of Hindu deities is not only limited to Vajrayana tradition but also in Theravada tradition in Sri Lanka where they use Indra, the king of devas as protector of dharma.

Conclusion

Nepal has a time-honoured tradition of art and culture embedded with Buddhism. In fact, the artistic tradition of Nepalese peoples is instrumental in elevating the status of Nepal in the world. In the past Nepalese artists produced many excellent images and were sent to Tibet, China, Japan and Mongolia. The bronze statue of Buddha Akshobhya Vajra (in Lhasa at Ramoche temple) is considered to be one of the most excellent images ever produced by the artists of Nepal, which was taken to Lhasa by Nepalese princess Bhrikuti Devi in the seventh century.

Although the artistic heritage has come a long way through the lives and lifestyle of Nepalese people, the exact meanings and implications as regard to the different images or deities relating to Vajrayana Buddhism has slowly gone out of focus during the passage of time. Even today there are many sculptors, artists and painters who can meticulously carve or paint such images or deities with excellent results, but the incumbent meanings however cannot be found with ease.

The purpose of this monograph is to provide some facts, materials and information on Buddhist Iconography gathered through extensive study of canonical texts relating to Vajrayana Buddhism prevailing in Nepal and some from Tibet albeit in a humble way. The readers are specifically sculptors, artists, painters and students of Buddhism interested in Buddhist Iconography and general public people. The monograph describes important deities and images specially relevant in Nepalese context along with their functions, utility, virtues and wisdom in the path to enlightenment.

7

Different Characteristics of Buddha in Nepal

DHARMAKAYA REPRESENTATION

Swayambhu

Nepal was the place where the system of Adi-buddha was originated. The Swayambhu Purana gives an account of the first manifestation of Adi-Buddha or primordial Buddha in the form of a flame of fire or Clear Light (*skt. Prabhashvara*). The meaning of Clear Light is self-cognizant and unfabricated original wakefulness primordially present in the mind stream of all sentient beings of the three realms. Since it is primordially present in all sentient beings it is called Buddha-nature or Tathagatagarbha or Adi-Buddha. The nature of Clear Light, which is Dharmakaya is not generally represented in images or sculptures. For Dharmakaya is not the form body. Dharmakaya aspect is depicted in a stupa or in a Caitya form only. However in Tibetan Nyingmapa tradition, Dharmakaya aspect is depicted in painting as Adi-Buddha Samantabhadra/ Samantabhadri form.

Samantabhadra is blue in color, symbolizing emptiness essence of our mind and Samantabhadri is white in color symbolizing clear knowing aspect of the mind. The unity of emptiness and cognizant aspect is thus depicted in male and female form of Adi-Buddha. Adi-Buddha does not mean first Buddha or creator of the Universe. Samantabhadri is totally nude and without even ornaments symbolizing Dharmakaya or the nature of the mind which is free of thought constructs or fabrication. It means that Dharmakaya can be realized only when we are free from thought constructs and perceive the emptiness nature of our mind directly.

SAMBHOGAKAYA REPRESENTATION

Vajradhara

Shakyamtini Buddha appeared in this world with the sole purpose of benefiting all sentient beings. Out of great compassion Lord Buddha revealed many different means/paths to enlightenment and set forth three Wheels of Law to suit varying degrees of intelligence and receptivities.

Shakyamuni Buddha himself was, it is said, in the form of Vajradhara while he was teaching tantric path to his gifted disciples. Vajradhara is depicted holding a Vajra and a bell in his left hand and his arms are kept crossed in front of him expressing complete integration of Prajna and Upaya. He is usually depicted in blue colour in vajraparyanka posture. He has a crown, an Urna and an Ushnisha as a Sambhogakaya Buddha.

Vajradhara is also depicted in father-mother (Aaju-Aji in Newari) aspect. Then he holds his usual symbols while his arms are crossed at the back of his consort. The consort is none other than Prajnaparamita in deified form.

The Kargyudpa lineage of Tibetan Buddhism begins with the Buddha Vajradhara. The individual in this tradition is allowed to visualize his root Guru as Buddha Vajradhara. Guru Tilopa is said to have received Mahamudra instruction directly from Buddha Vajradhara through visions and other extraordinary means.

In Nispannayogavali, Vajradhara is the main deity in Vajrasattvamandala. He is three faced, six-armed and reddish white in color. His right arm holds a vajra, a sword and a kapala and his left hand holds a bell, an ankush and a noose. He stands in the Ardhaparyanka posture and dances in Tandava style.

Vajrasattva

Vajrasattva is also regarded as Adi-Buddha by Nepalese Vajracharyas who follow Vajrayana tradition according to the text Vajrasattvakaya. His body is white with one face and two hands. His right hand holds a five-pronged golden vajra at his heart. His left hand holds a silver bell at his side. He sits in the Vajraparyanka posture wearing precious silks and ornaments with jewel diadem.

His body is adorned with 32 major and 80 minor marks of a Sambhogakaya and emits a clear limitless light. It appears to lack all notion of substantiality, like the reflection of moon in water.

Vajrasattva has father-mother aspect too. Generally this form is not exhibited in open. It is shown only to those who are initiated in Highest Yoga Tantra. His form is the same as in the single one but his consort carries a kartri in her right hand and a kapala in her left hand.

Vajrasattva is said to have been originated from seed syllable *Hum* and is generally invoked for removal of obscuration of Kleshavarana and Jneyavarana. His hundred syllable mantra is very efficacious in purifying our defilements through confession practice. It is said if confession is done with the four opponent powers, then non-virtuous actions or obscurations will be purified. The first opponent power is the force of reliance. This means looking upon the visualized image of Vajrasattva as the embodiment of one's refuge. The second opponent power is the sincere regret for the non-virtuous action done by one-self The third opponent power is desisting from evil deeds. The fourth opponent power is to apply power of good deeds; and specially regarding this case, practicing the meditation and recitation of Vajrasattva without parting from Bodhicitta while remaining in the state of emptiness. Vajrasattva is a very popular tutelary deity for Nepalese Vajracaryas. He is worshipped very often by Nepalese Buddhists through Gurumandala ritual.

Vairocana Buddha

He is one of the five Tathagatas symbolizing all pervasive wisdom (*skt. Suvisuddha dharma dhatu jnana*) i.e. knowledge free from all kinds of obscuration. He is placed generally in the sanctum of the stupa. Sometimes he is placed between Akshobhya and Ratna Sambhava in the stupa. He resides always in the Akanistha heaven.

He is white in color and his hands are held against his chest with the tips of thumb and forefinger of each hand joined displaying Bodhyanga mudra. His vehicle is a pair of lions symbolizing lions roar of dharmadhatujnana which terrifies all wrong views. He can be recognized through white disc or dharmacakra, which cuts all wrong views.

Vairocana Buddha originates from the seed syllable *Om* placed on the orb of the moon. He also represents Rupa (form) of five aggregates. He is not a historical Buddha like Shakyamuni Buddha. According to Dharmalakshana sect of Mahayana Buddhism he is considered to be Svabhavika-kaya of Shakyamuni Buddha. In some esoteric sect of Japan he is said to be the supreme lord of secret vehicle i.e. Mahavairocana.

When Vairocana Buddha is four faced and eight-armed he is addressed as Vajradhatu Buddha. According to Vajradhatumandala of Nispannayogavali, Vairocana is seated in Vajraparyanka and is white in color. His four faces are of white, yellow, red, and green color. He is eight-armed with his two hands holding a vajra and displaying dharmacakra mudra; the second pair shows dhyana mudra, third pair holds a rosary and an arrow and the last pair holds a discus and a bow.

Akshobhya Buddha

He is also one of the five Tathagatas symbolizing Mirror like Wisdom (*skt. Adarsa jnana*), which means the wisdom like space, all pervasive, without periphery and without characteristics. He is the essence of purified form of Hatred. As in a mirror every visible object reflects so the knowledge of dharmakaya reflects in our mind. The image of Akshobhya Buddha is generally placed in the East in the stupa.

He is blue in color. He exhibits Earth-touching gesture (*skt. bhumisparsa mudra*). He rides on the throne of an elephant symbolizing steadfast nature of his bodhisattva vows. In the past when he was a bodhisattva he made these strong vows in front of Buddha Mahacakshu.

a) I now engender supreme bodhicitta. If I bear malice against sentient beings from now until my attainment of supreme enlightenment I will be disobeying all the Buddhas.

b) Now I have resolved to pursue All Knowing Wisdom and firmly dedicated to this goal. If I generate any doubt, intention to kill or steal, any wrong view or impure deed or if I am prone to lying, duplicity or harsh language or if I hurt other in other ways from now on until my attainment of supreme enlightenment, I will be deceiving Buddhas.

When he thus first brought forth bodhicitta, this bodhisattvamahasattva was clad with the armour of vigor, and was never moved by hatred or the like toward any sentient being. Since then, because of his thought, the Bodhisattva was called Akshobhya the immovable of the land of Abhirati.

In other words, Akshobhya attained Buddhahood under the tree of seven jewels in the land of Abhirati i.e. wonderful joy in the east. Because of the power of his vows, there are no lower realms in his Buddha land. Every sentient being in his Buddha land does virtuous deeds and restrains from angry behaviours. According to the Ratnakuta Sutra, if one determines to practice the bodhisattva way of life, as he vows be will be reborn in that Abhirati Buddhaland. It is said that the famous Upasaka Vimalakirti is the person transformed from the land of Abhirati Buddhaland.

Ratna Sambhava Buddha

He is one of five Tathagatas symbolzing wisdom of equality (*skt. Samatajnana*). According to the commentary of Namasangiti, the author Ravisri says;

"All the phenomena is devoid of essence, lacks true inherent existence and hence is dream like or illusion or is empty".

Thus the knowledge of essencelessness of persons and the phenomena is the wisdom of equality: Buddha Ratnasambhava is the personification of this wisdom in Vajrayana Buddhism.

In the extant literature he is rarely described about his vows, aspirations and activity. He is usually called the Buddha born form jewel.

He is yellow in color. He belongs to the Buddha family of Jewel. He is placed in the stupa facing to the south. He shows varada mudra with his right hand. He holds cintamani jewel in his left hand kept on his lap. He also represents the purified form of the defilement pride. He rides on the horse throne symbolizing that he ferries over the suffering sentient beings with full vigor. He resides in the pure abode of Ratnavati heaven (buddha field).

It is said that when Ratna Sambhava Buddha attained enlightenment golden colored rays emitted from his crown and manifested limitless golden colored bodhisattvas; each one of them carrying jeweled scepters emitting light shining on the southern worlds, which were numerous as the sands of the Ganges.

It is said that the sentient beings wish would be fulfilled when one sees the golden colored light. It is also said that by meditating on Ratna Sambhava Buddha's body, one's desire would be fulfilled.

Amitabha Buddha

Amitabha Buddha is also one of the five Tathagatas representing the wisdom of discriminating awareness (*skt. Pratyavekshanajnana*). When discriminating wisdom dawns on us we realize Non-production or non-origination of all things. He also represents purified form of desire.

Amitabha Buddha is red in color. He is represented in the stupa facing to the west. He rides on peacock symbolizing that he can take away the suffering of others just as the peacock eats poisonous plants and yet his tail shines forth.

Amitabha in Sanskrit means immeasurable light or limitless light. He resides in the western land of unlimited bliss (*skt. Sukhavati*). He is assisted by two bodhisattvas viz. Avalokiteshvara and Mahasthamprapta.

When he was a bodhisattva he was called Bhikshu Dharmakara. He made 48 vows to establish an adorned land of unlimited bliss to ferry over those living beings who recite his name. On the basis of those vows, any living being who has faith, makes vows and practices diligently will be received by this Buddha and reborn in the pure land of unlimited bliss.

Amitabha Buddha presides over the Bhadrakalpa i.e. Fortunate Aeon. He always exhibits Dhyana mudra. He belongs to the Lotus family. He originates from, the seed syllable *Hrih*. He can be recognized through the symbol of the lotus.

With his extensive vows and great compassion this Buddha has ferried over innumerable sentient beings. The recitation of the name of Amitabha Buddha is a common practice in China and Japan. In Tibet too, devotees recite very often the prayer to he reborn in the land of Amitabha Buddha.

Among Siddhi Buddha

Amoghsiddhi Buddha is the last among the Five Buddhas. He represents the All Accomplishing Wisdom (*skt. Krityanusthan jnana*). He also represents the purified form of jealosy. When one realizes All Accomplishing Wisdom one can perform all the Buddha activity without pre-meditation. This happens spontaneously.

Amoghsiddhi is green in colour. He is represented in the stupa facing to the north. He rides on Garuda symbolizing that he can detect the presence of serpent-like delusion from a distance. A serpent with seven hoods and an umbrella is depicted on the background. He exhibits abhayamudra showing that by following bodhisattva path fearlessness is gained.

Like Ratna Sambhava Buddha, the vows, activity and deeds of Amogh Siddhi Buddha are not extant in Mahayana Buddhist literature. It is however said that cultivators relying on this Buddha's protection will achieve accomplishments in Buddhist affairs and worldly matters and will perfect the work benefiting sentient beings.

Amogh Siddhi Buddha alone has a canopy of snakes over his head. He sometimes resembles Shakyamuni Buddha with nine headed Naga king Mucalinda in paintings.

According to tantric text, this Buddha is said to be originated from seed syllable green *Khan*: He is also said to be the embodiment of volition (*skt. Sanskara*) and Air element (*skt. Vayu*).

Bhaisajyaguru Vaiduryaprabha Tathagata (Medicine Buddha)

Bhaisajya Tathagata is called Healing Buddha or Medicine Buddha. He is able to cure the sickness of birth and death. His body is bright, like lapislazuli. He resides in the eastern world of purified lapislazuli. He is assisted by two bodhisattvas called Sutyaprabha and Candraprabha, to transform and teach living beings in that land.

The usual colour of Bhaisajya Tathagata was blue or lapislazuli in colour. But he had also golden colour. His right hand held a branch of the myrobalan in varadamudra gesture. His left hand is in the lap holding a pindapatra (alms bowl).

The blue or lapislazuli color of this body symbolizes that he takes all the diseases and sickness of the suffering beings unto himself. The plant myrobalan signifies the medicine, which heals all the sickness of sentient beings.

According to the Bhaisajyaguru Buddha Sutra, he made 12 great vows before his attainment of Buddhahood. The important vows are as follows: to eliminate sickness from all living beings and make them feel easy and happy in order to attain Buddhahood; and to liberate beings from disasters and calamities. It is said that the land of Bhaisajya Buddha is genuinely pure. In that land the ground is paved with purified lapislazuli. The cities, buildings and palaces are made of seven jewels. In that land the sentient beings do not commit any evil deeds hence there is no lower realm. It can well be compared with Sukhavati Heaven of Buddha Amitabha.

In Tibetan medical tradition Bhaisajya Buddha is said to be the source of all medical treatises. This Buddha is invoked for eliminating disasters and sickness of all varieties.

Amitayus or Buddha Aparimita

Buddha Aparimita is very popular in bestowing long life upon the devotees. He is red in colour. His two hands are in dhyana mudra and holds an ambrosia vase (*skt. Amrit kalasha*). He usually wears all the ornaments of different kinds peculiar to a Sambhogakaya Buddha. He is never depicted with any consort. He wears a crown and has Ushnisha and Urnakosh in his body.

Buddha Aparimira is invoked or worshipped for lengthening the life span or fast relief from dreadful diseases or from mortal danger. In Nepalese Mahayana tradition the dharani of Buddha Aparimita is often recited by the devotees in the presence of dying patients. The recitation of this dharani is said to be efficacious when carried out in utter sincerity. It is said that the famous Madhayamika Buddhist philosopher Arya Nagarjuna had escaped his early death after recitation of this dharani for one complete day and night.

Buddha Durgatiparisodhanaraja

When the Buddha Shakyamuni enters into a special type of samadhi called Sarvadurgatiparisodhana i.e. elimination of all evil destinies, it is called Buddha Durgatiparisodhanaraja. This sculpture is really very rare. But there are many paintings of this deity in Nepal.

He is yellow in colour. He exhibits Dharmacakramudra and has one face and two arms only. He is described in the Durgatisodhana mandala of Nispannayogavali. His dharani is very popular among Nepalese Buddhists and it is very often recited in front of a dead body or in funeral ceremonies. At the request of Devaraja Indra, Buddha Shakyamuni, our of compassion for the deva Vimalamaniprabha, who was reborn in Avici Hell, delivered the dharani of Durgatiparisodhana which can liberate beings from the hells like Avici.

8

Nirmanakaya Representation in Buddhist Tradition

Buddha Dipamkara

In Buddhist tradition the Buddhas of three times is often mentioned. The Pali Buddhavamsa counts 24 Past Buddhas, including Dipamkara as the first. While in Mahayana Buddhist tradition the number of Buddhas increases much more. The Sarvastivada tradition counts 75,000 Buddhas commencing with Shakyamuni and ends before Buddha Ratnasikhin during the First Asamkheya Kalpa. During the second Asamkheya Kalpa, 76,000 Buddhas from Buddha Ratnasikhin to Dipamkara and during the third Asamkheya 77,000 Buddhas from Dipamkara to Vipasyin Buddha are counted.

Buddha Dipamkara is represented widely in Kathmandu valley. Especially in the month of the Gunla Festival many large sized images in bronze and copper are displayed in Nepalese Buddhist monasteries. In the Samyak festival Buddha Dipamkara is the chief deity to be displayed and worshipped.

The Buddha Dipamkara is usually yellow in colour and exhibits abhayamudra and varada mudra with his two hands.

It is believed that Shakyamuni Buddha started his bodhisattva career after meeting with Buddha Dipamkara. When Buddha Dipamkara was visiting the city of Dipavati, a young brahman versed in vedic lore happened to pass by the city of Dipavati fully decorated with hanners and in festive mood to honor Buddha Dipamkara. He also happened to meet a young brahman girl with seven lotus flowers, going to honor Lord Dipamkara. The learned Brahman Megha asked the lady to give him seven lotus flowers for 500 gold coins. But she refused and agreed to give him five flowers under the condition that she can become his wife until he attained enlightenment. After that Megha Brahman saw Buddha

Dipamkara from a distance. Identifying himself with Buddha Dipamkara he made a strong vow that he will become a Buddha in future. Thrilled and inspired after seeing the Buddha he threw five lotus flowers in a prayer and the young girl who was to become Yasodhara also threw two flowers in the same manner. These seven lotus flowers formed a garland and floated in the air around the Buddha's head in a miraculous way. Later on Buddha Dipamkara too, prophesied that he would be a Buddha Shakyamuni in future.

Buddha Vipashvi

Buddha Vipashvi is said to have planted the seed of lotus from Nagarjuna hill, on a big lake called Nagadaha (now Kathmandu valley). At that time Satyadharma Bodhisattva, who was to become Shakyamuni Buddha, was accompanying Vipashvi Buddha. Lord Vipashvi Buddha threw a lotus seed into the lake. When his disciples asked why he did so, Lord Vipashvi Buddha explained that there would appear a self-originated divine light, a manifestation of Primordial Buddha from Akanistha Bhuvan and people would call it Swayambhu.

He also predicted that in the future Bodhisattva Manjushree will drain the water off from the valley and make it a habitable land. The Jatamatrochcha hill is thus blessed by lord Vipashvi Buddha. A big white caitya was constructed there to commemorate the visit of lord Vispashvi Buddha. On the memory of planting of lotus seed by Vipashvi Buddha a festival is held even today in the month of March every year.

Lord Vipashvi was born in the city of Bandhumati, ninety-one aeons (Kalpa) ago. His parents were Bandhuman and Bandhumati. His wife was Sutan. Samvattakhanda was his son. He enjoyed his worldly life for 8,000 years. He practiced the austerities for 8 months after his great renunciation. His Mahaparinirvana took place at the age of 80,000 years in Sunittaramna. His sculptures are not genereally available. But usually he is depicted in bhumisparsa mudra and with yellow or golden color.

Sikhi Buddha

Sikhi Buddha was born in Arunavati, 31 aeons ago according to textual sources. His parents were Aruna and Prabhavati. His wife was Sabbakama and his son was Atula. He was called Sikhi because his Usnisa stood up like sikha (flame). He enjoyed the worldly life for 7,000 years. After his Mahabhiniskramana i.e. great renunciation, he practiced penance for eight months. He attained enlightenment under the foot of a pundarika tree. His body was sixty cubits in height. His great parinirvana took place in Silavati at the age of 70,000 years. During his lifetime he visited Swayambhu Ksetra knowing that a self-originated divine light had appeared over a beautifully bloomed thousand petalled lotus. He came with his disciples including Kshemaraja Grihapati who was to become Shakyamuni Buddha later on. Sikhi Buddha is said to have composed a hymn in praise of lord Swayambhu and mingled himself with lord Swayambhu. According to Swayambhu Purana, Buddha Sikhi predicted that from the root of the lotus an image of Nairatmya devi would appear. The discourse with such prediction took place on Dhyanochcha Mountain of Kathmandu valley. He is usually depicted in abhayamudra.

Buddha Bishvabhu

Buddha Bishvabhu was born in the city of Anuparam/Anoma. His parents were the king Sujita and Queen Yasavati. His wife was Sucitta and his son Suppa Buddha. He enjoyed his wordly life for six thousand years. After his great renunciation he practiced the penance for six months. He attained enlightenment under the Sala tree. At that time Bodhisattva Parvatakshya who was to become Shakyamuni later, was with Bishvabhu Buddha. He came to pay homage to Swayambhu with this bodhisattva. Buddha Bishvabhu offered 125,000 flowers from the eastern mountain called Fullochcha now called Fulchowk.

Buddha Bislivabhu also predicted that the Kathmandu valley would have many sacred power places (*skt. tirtha and vitaraga*). At the base of this mountain a fountain from of stream will appear and those who desire water will get it there.

Buddha Bishvabhu remained in this world for 60,000 years and passed away in Nirvana at the place called Khomarama. He is depicted in Dharmacakramudra.

Buddha Krakuchchanda

Buddha Krakuchchanda was the first buddha of the current aeon which is called Fortunate Aeon (skt. Bhadrakalpa). According to the Bhadrakalpika Sutra it is said that one thousand Buddhas would appear in succession. The present Buddha Shakyamuni is the fourth.

Buddha Krakuchchanda was born in the city of Ksemavati. His parents were brahmana Agnidutta and Visakha Visvacini Devi. His wife was Virocamana and his son was Uttara. He enjoyed his worldy life for 4,000 years. After his great renunciation he practiced penance for eight months. He attained supreme enlightenment at the foot of Sirisa tree. He gave his first sermon to 84,000 monks near the city of Makila. In the course of his buddha activity he visited Kathmandu valley to pay homage to lord Swayambhu with his disciples including the king of Saketa Dharmapala the priest Gunadhoj brahmana and many others. At that time, Jyotipala Bodhisattva, who was to become Shakyamuni later, was serving the Buddha Krakuchchanda with great faith and devotion. The Buddha Krakuchchanda after paying homage to lord Swayambhu and Nairatmya Devi, ascended on the Siddhifullochcha hill i.e. Northern hill of Kathmandu valley, popularly known these days as Shivapuri Hill.

The Buddha Krakuchchanda gave many different kinds of teachings on Hinayana, Mahayana and Vajrayana. He delivered specially 37 factors of enlightenment in this mountain area. Seven hundred monks were given initiation. At that time there were no traces of water. The Buddha Krakuchchanda through his miraculous utterance issued forth a stream of water and hence the name Bagmati. He is depicted in varadamudra with the left hand holding the fold of the robe.

Buddha Kanakamuni

Buddha Kanakamuni (also called Konagamana) was the second Buddha of this Bhadrakalpa. He was born in Shobhavati. His parents were brahmana Yakshadutta and Uttarani. His wife was Rucigatta and his son was Sarthavaha. He enjoyed this worldly pleasure for three thousand years. After his renunciation he practiced his austerities for six months. He attained his supreme enlightenment at the foot of an Udumbara tree. His first sermon was attended by 30,000 monks near Sudarsana Nagara. His body was 30 cubits high. He passed away at the Pabbatarama at the age of 30,000 years.

During his career Buddha Kanakamuni also visited Swayambhu Kshetra in Kathmandu valley. After his Parinirvana, a stupa was erected near Kapilavastu at Niglihawa in the Western Terai region of Nepal. This has been confirmed by the Ashokan inscription.

Buddha Kanakamuni is generally represented as yellow in colour. His right hand has Abhayamudra and his left hand is in dhyana mudra.

Buddha Kasyapa

Buddha Kasyapa was the third Buddha of this fortunate aeon. He was born in the city of Benaras. He was from brahman family. His parents were Brahmadutta and Dhanavati. His wife was Sunanda and his son Vijitasena. He enjoyed this worldly life for two thousand years. He practiced the penance only for seven days. He attained supreme enlightenment under the Banyan tree. He gave his first sermon to 10 million monks. His body was 20 cubits high. He passed away at Sotavya in Benaras at the age of 20,000 years.

During his buddha activity he also visited Swayambhu Ksetra to pay homage to Swayambhu Mahacaitya. At that time Jyoti Raj Bodhisattva, who was to become Shakyamuni Buddha, was following Buddha Kasyapa along with such chief disciples as Tisya, Uttama and Sotthita. After performing homage to lord Swayambhu he returned to his country. He then went to Gaud (Orissa?). In that city there lived a pious king Prachanda Deva, who used to subdue his enemies and appreciated the deeds of the sage. After obtaining blessings and instructions from Kasyapa Tathagata he went to Kathmandu renouncing his kingdom. King Prachanda Deva paid homage to lord Swayambhu and became a disciple of Acarya Gunakara. Acarya Gunakara ordained and initiated him in the mysteries of Sutras and Tantras. He was then called Santikar Acarya. Acarya Santikar, thinking of the later periods, when people with evil mind might destroy this self-originated divine light, decided to cover it by erecting a stupa over it. Bhikshu Gunakara gave him permission to construct a stupa and conferred on him the title of Vajracharya. After completing the stupa he went to the retreat in Santipur.

Buddha Kashyapa is always depicted as yellow in colour. His right hand shows Varada mudra and the left hand is in dhyana mudra. He always sits on a lion throne with a lotus.

Buddha Shakyamuni

Buddha Shakyaniuni is the fourth Buddha of this fortunate aeon. As he has realized the potential of his inner being and has removed all the obscurations and has developed all the positive qualities, he is called a Buddha, a fully Awakened one. Of countless Buddhas who have appeared and will continue to appear on this earth, Buddha Shakyamuni was the one who regenerated the teachings of enlightened beings for our present era.

Shakyamuni Buddha was born in Kapilavasto in Nepal some 2,600 years ago and performed many buddha activities, for 45 years in this Indian sub-continent, for the benefit of all sentient beings. His most outstanding deed were the teachings, which showed the path to liberation from the suffering of birth and death to the supreme enlightenment of Buddhahood. This is symbolized by Dharmacakra mudra of the Buddha. Buddha Shakyamuni out of compassion for all sentient beings taught many different kinds of teachings, mostly sutras and tantras to suit the varying degrees of intelligence of his disciples.

All the Sutra and Tantra teachings of the Buddha Shakyamuni are said to be the means of liberation or the path leading to Buddhahood. According to Swayambhu Purana, Buddha Shakyamuni also visited Swayambhu Caitya and delivered the teachings on the origin of Swayambhu Stupa upon the request of Bodhisattva Maitreya.

The images of Buddha Shakyamuni can be found in large numbers carved in various materials like stone, metals, claywire, or in paintings or other forms. He is depicted in various postures. Most popular Buddha images found in Nepal are in Bhumisparsa mudra i.e. earth touching gesture with yellow robe. He has Usnisha, on the crown of the head, Urnakosha between eyebrows and long lobed ears. He is golden in color. He has 32 major and 80 minor marks of Sambhogakaya Buddha. He is always seen with pinda patra (alms bowl) over the hand on the lap. He can also be seen in vitarka mudra, dhyana mudra, dharmacakramudra, and other mudras.

9
Buddhist Gurus in Nepal

Guru Nagarjuna

Guru Nagarjuna lived in India 2,000 years ago. He flourished in the second half of the second century of the Christian era. He was a contemporary friend of the Satavahana king Gautamiputra Yajnasri (166-196 A.D.). He came from a wealthy brahmin family from Vidarbha. He went to Nalanda where he became a disciple of the great sage Rahula Bhadra and underwent a thorough training in all five branches of learning.

After his ordination he remained for sometime a monk of Sarvastivada and later changed into Mahayana. In the course of his career as a wandering monk he came across a treatise of Prajnaparamita Sutras. He composed a series of treatise on Madhyamika philosophy based on Prajnaparamita Sutras. His six works on Madhyamika philosophy are well known to the Buddhist world. They are as follows: I. Mula Madhyamika Sastra, 2. Sunyata Saptati, 3. Yukti Sastika, 4. Vigrahavyavartani, 5. Ratnavali, 6. Vaidalyaprakaran.

Nagarjuna developed a system of philosophy called Madhyamika based on the Buddha's original sutras. He expounded the true meaning of sunyata based on four point analysis (*skt. Catuskoti*). According to him all the phenomena and the person have no true existence of their own. They are all dependently originated and cannot have their independent existence.

To realize Nirvana, according to him is to realize Emptiness in all its depth. Later on his philosophy was nurtured and enhanced by Arya Deva, Candrakirti, Buddhapalita and Acarya Santi Deva. The Vajrayana doctrine of Nepal is usually based on Madhyamika as well as Yogacara doctrines.

In its sculpture and paintings Nagarjuna is seen as a bodhisattva with nine serpents around his head. He is generally seen in Dharmacakra mudra i.e. teaching mudra symbolizing teaching of the doctrine of emptiness to all sentient beings in order to eliminate ego-grasping. He wears a saffron coloured robe and sits on a cushion proper for a dharma master.

Guru Padma Sambhava

Guru Padma Sambhava is popularly known as Guru Rinpoche, the precious teacher. He was a powerful Tantric Buddhist Master who was invited to Tibet in the eighth century to diffuse the Buddhism in Tibet. He subdued many harmful influences and forces that hindered the spread of compassionate teachings of Buddha Shakyamuni. Through his miraculous powers and enlightened experiences, he taught many disciples who came out to be perfect masters of Tantric Buddhism. He is said to have twenty-five great disciples who were instrumental in preserving the sacred teachings of Lord Buddha till today; through their various manifestations.

Guru Rinpoche is said to have eight manifestations called Guru Tsangye in peaceful and wrathful postures. Through them he caused Vajrayana dharma to spread widely in Nepal, India, Bhutan and Tibet. Guru Rinpoche is revered as founder of Nyingma or ancient tradition of Tibetan Buddhism. Tibetans believe Guru Rinpoche is no different from Shakyamuni Buddha himself.

Guru Rinpoche's body is depicted as golden in color. His hat is usually red. So Nyingmapa is generally called red hat sect of Tibetan Buddhism. He wears different robes of differing colors symbolizing his enlightened experiences and attainments. His inner garment is white symbolizing clear light aspect of his mind and the outer garment is of a red color, which means he has deep and great compassion for all sentient beings. His outermost coat is brown symbolizing his renunciation. He is seated upon a lotus of alternating blue with red and green with orange petals.

Guru Nropa

Guru Naropa lived in India about 900 years ago. He was a great learned man versed in Sutras, Tantras and many other ancient lores. During his stay in the famous Nalanda monastery his intellectual accomplishment was foremost and without any match. But his intellectual pride was humbled by an old lady who was an emanation of Vajrayogini. At that time, she also suggested him to consult Guru Tilopa for the real understanding of Mahamudra.

Naropa searched for Guru Tilopa exerting much effort. His arduous search and devotion to Guru Tilopa has become a legend in itself. Naropa found Guru Tilopa by the bank of a river. He was dressed like a mad man and was eating fish, which was unusual for a holy man. Naropa underwent training under him for about twelve years and received the inner transmission of Mahamudra practice. The profound Mahamudra teachings was received by Guru Tilopa directly from Buddha Vajradhara. Naropa is generally dressed in the white lower garments of a yogi. His body is of an ash colour like that of a wandering mendicant. His left hand holds a skull cup filled with nectar and his right hand shows varada mudra. He sits in Lalitasana posture under an antilope mat. He wears a meditation band on his waist.

Guru Atisha

Guru Atisha is popularly known as Acarya Dipamkarasrijnana. He lived some 1,000 years ago (982-1054 A.D.). He was born in a royal family of Bengal. From a very young age he studied and mastered many scriptural texts on various subjects. He went to Sumatra, an arduous journey lasting for 13 months, to meet the illustrious master of Bodhisattva tradition honoured and respected as Guru Suvarnadvipa. He received teachings on Mind Training in completeness.

He was invited to Tibet to eliminate all the mistakes and misunderstanding concerning the teachings of Hinayana, Mahayana and Tantrayana. He established Kadampa sect in Tibet through his Tibetan disciple Drontonpa.

Guru Atisha is generally seen seated in Vajra posture with dharmacakra mudra. A Kadam style stupa is usually seen on his right side symbolizing awakened mind and the stages of path to Enlightenment.

Guru Marpa

Guru Marpa was the founder of Kagyudpa tradition of Tibetan Buddhism. He was born in 1012 A.D. in the region of Lobrak, Tibet, right above the border of Bhutan. In his childhood he quickly learned reading and writing. He learnt Sanskrit from Drogmi Lotsava who was well versed in Path and Fruition doctrine of Sakyapa tradition. Having been frustrated with his inability to learn more teachings from Drogmi he toured India three times via Nepal. Guru Marpa had two Nepali Gurus, Paindapa and Chitherpa from whom he learnt the Cakrasamvara and Catuhpith tantras for three years. These two Nepalese teachers gave Guru Marpa a great deal of dharma instruction and language. Guru Marpa with his great zeal and assiduity learnt the vast range of tantric teachings from Naropa, Maitripa, Kukkuripa and others. He came back to Tibet with these vast resources and taught his disciples extensively. Among his disciples, Tibet's great yogi Milarepa was the foremost and he had many outstanding disciples of his own through whom Kagyudpa lineage is continued uninterruptedly till today.

Guru Marpa is said to be a very fat one with hair standing five fingers straight up off his head and with angry looking face. But in some commentaries of Venerable Karma Chagme, he is described as having matted hair and wearing a chuba with big Chinese style sleeves and a large cap.

Guru Milarepa

Guru Milarepa is believed to be the most beloved and highly accomplished Buddhist master of Tibet. His songs on enlightened experiences are still sung today by the learned and lay people alike. Guru Milarepa during his early career committed many evil deeds through black magic, and sending hailstorms too. He later regretted his evil deeds and eventually found his worthy and enlightened Guru Marpa, who put him on trials and hardships in other to test his guru devotion and eagerness to practice dharma teachings. He later conferred on him the series of empowerments and essential teachings of Mahamudra, which he received from Guru Naropa. Guru Milarepa meditated on these tantric teachings with great zeal in wild and forlorn mountains for 6 years and eventually achieved the realization ofVajradharahood in his very lifetime.

Millions of devotees took inspiration from his practice and verification of Buddhist teachings.

Guru Milarepa is generally seen in a cotton-clad dress seated on antilope skin with Lalitasana posture. He wears a meditation band. His right hand is generally put on the ears symbolizing that he is listening to the voices of beings in lower realms. He has great compassion for them and sentient beings in general. His body is usually blue or green in colour. It is said that during his meditation he ate nothing but nettles for the long period of time and his skin thus assumed a greenish hue. Sometimes to represent his realizations, his body is depicted golden in color too.

Guru Tson Khapa

Guru Tson Khapa appeared in Tibet in the fourteenth century as the great revitalizer of Tibetan Buddhism. He is also known as Je Rinpoche. He is believed to be the manifestation of Guru Rinpoche himself. Guru Tson Khapa emphasized the value of discipline in monastic institutions and the value of academic pursuits and practice. He founded the Gelugpa tradition and among his closest disciple was Gedun Drub, later known as the First Dalai Lama.

Guru Tson Khapa popularized the theme of Lamrim i.e. Stages of the path to Enlightenment introduced in Tibet by Guru Atisha. He is said to be the emanation of Bodhisattva Manjushree. He is shown holding a sword and a hook. His body is radiant white with reddish glow. He sits upon sun and moon discs in lotus throne. He wears the traditional monastic robes and is crowned with a pandit yellow hat.

Guru Sakya Pandit

Guru Sakya Pandit is said to be one of the three manifestation of Manjushree - the other two being the great Nyingma Lama Long Chen Rabjampa and Gelugpa Lama Guru Tson Khapa.

Guru Sakya Pandit was an immensely learned lama versed in five branches of learning. In Tibet he was recognized as master debater at par with Indian Guru Dharmakirti. He vanquished all his opponents, both buddhists and non-buddhists in debate. On hearing the erudition of Sakya Pandit, Mongol Prince Godan invited him to his capital. Since then the abbots of Shakya monastery entered into a new era in the Tibetan political scenario. (1270-1340).

Guru Sakya Pandit propagated the system of Path and Fruit doctrine (*skt. Margaphala siddhant*). Being an emanation of Manjushree he is also generally depicted holding a sword and a book.

10

Great Eight Bodhisattvas of Nepal

Samantabhadra Bodhisattva

Amongst the bodhisattvas of the high rank Samantabhadra stands prominent. His activities are mentioned in Gandavyuha sutra. His most popular practice, known as Samantabhadra Carya, is a household name for the Nepalese Buddhist.

Samantabhadra is represented with a crown, ornaments and princely garments of a bodhisattva typical of Sambhogakaya aspect. He holds Cintamani in his left hand and supports a blue lotus at his left shoulder. His right hand displays vitarka mudra. His posture may be either seated or standing. In Nispannayogavali, he is described as yellow in colour, showing the varadamudra in his right hand and holding the sword on lotus on his left hand.

He is also depicted as golden-yellow in colour. He holds a bunch of jewels in the right hand and the left hand rests on the hip. According to a legend concerning Samantabhadra, it is said that Kathmandu valley was once a great lake measuring 14 km by 14 km in size. At the center of this lake blossomed a thousand petalled lotus where there was a flame of self-existing wisdom i.e. Swayambhu. Many sages and devas used to bathe in this lake and pay homage to Lord Swayambhu. Knowing that a self-existing Buddha had appeared in the lake Lord Manju Deva Acarya, an emanation of Bodhisattva Manjushree, from Wu-tai-shan mountain of Great China, came to Kathmandu to drain water from the lake so as to make it a habitable land as the legend narrates. This act of Manjudeva Acarya enraged Kulika Nagaraja who began to obstruct its outlets thus ponding water once again into the lake. As a result, many people suffered due to floods and destruction of houses. The people began to take refuge in Lord Avalokiteshvara for protection. In the mean time Avalokiteshvara Bodhisattva sent

Samantabhadra Bodhisattva for the purpose of relieving the sufferings of the people in Kathmandu. Samantabhadra subdued Kulika Naga and also inspired him to practice dharma and gave many blessings.

In Buddhist practice Samantabhadra Bodhisattva is very famous for his extensive ten great vows and seven fold worship. His grandeur is well presented in the Lotus sutra and Gandavyuha sutra.

Ksitigarbha Bodhisattva

Among the great eight Bodhisattvas, Ksitigarbha stands prominent for his great compassion and vows for the sake of suffering beings residing in hells. In the Buddhist Pantheon, he is one of the most highly celebrated bodhisattvas in the category of Manjushree, Avalokiteshvara, and Samantabhadra. These four represent the four basic qualities of the Buddha i.e. Manjushree for great wisdom; Avalokiteshyara for his great compassion; Samantabhadra for his great meritorious deeds, and Ksitigarbha for his great vows (to help and liberate all sentient beings residing in the hells). The famous pronouncement of Bodhisattva Ksitigarbha, "If I do not go to hell to help them there, who else will go?" is the manifestation of this profound vow.

Ksitigarbha is depicted wearing fivefold ornaments. He is in standing posture with his right hand in vitarka mudra and left hand in varada mudra. His symbol is the Cintamani jewel, which is in the shape of a flaming pearl, supported by a lotus flower. He is also represented in a seated position holding a staff with his two hands. In Sadhanamala he is of green colour and shows in his two hands the jar and Abhayamudra.

In Chinese Turkestan he is represented as a good judge of the infernal regions surrounded by ten kings of hells. He wears the usual headdress of which both ends hang over the shoulders, and carries an alarm staff to force open the gates of hell. In his left hand he holds the luminous pearl, which dispels the darkness of the hell regions. Below the lotus on which he is seated, is his vahana, a winged lion.

Ksitigarbha Bodhisattva through his miraculous powers appears throughout ten direction in an innumerable forms of transformed bodies in order to lead even the most obstinate and deluded living beings to follow the path of the Buddha. The essence of his great vows is the filial piety. To be filial to one's parents is the practice of filial piety. The filial practice of Ksitigarbha bodhisattva is not limited to one's parents but to all the sentient beings, who are infinite.

Akashgarbha or Khagarbha Bodhisattva

Khagarbha Bodhisattva is represented in standing posture with his hands in vitarka and varada mudra. His symbol is the sun upon a book. A graceful drapery falls from his waist and a long narrow scarf is tied around the body from the left shoulder to the right hip. His hair is drawn up in a stupa shaped ushnisha.

According to the Akashgarbha sutra, Lord Buddha has praised him highly thus 'His dhyana is as deep as the sea, his pure precept is as high as mountain, his wisdom is worthy of receiving the best offerings from all living beings. His merit and virtue are unsurpassed'. It is said that he is twenty yojana in height manifesting a great body. He wears a crown, which manifests 35 images of Buddhas of confession. His power of compassion is just like Avalokiteshvara. He benefits living beings continuously. It is said that when a beginner bodhisattva commits a crime and confesses just once before Akashgarbha Bodhisattva their evils will be eliminated and they will be purified immediately.

According to the Swayambhu legend, when Odiayana Acarya was meditating in a mountain near Swayambhu hill he desired to have a vision of Akashgarbha Bodhisattva and hence he blew a conch shell. In the meantime Akashgarbha Bodhisattva with a view to bless Odiayana Acarya appeared in front of him and gave many blessings to him. He manifested a stream of brilliant light and entered into a boulder and vanished. Akashgarbha Bodhisattva predicted then that he would be the famous Acarya Bandhudatta who would bring Arya Avalokiteshvara from Assam and conduct a chariot festival in the Kathmandu valley and gain liberation thereby at the feet of Arya Avalokiteshvara. So the place where Akashgarbha Bodhisattva issued forth a stream of light is called Adi-shvara near Swayambhu hill.

Sarvanivarana Vishkambhin

Bodhisattva Sarvanivarana Vishkambhin is also a celebrated Bodhisattva mentioned in the Guna Karandavyuha sutra who effaces all the sins of the devotees.

He is either blue or white in colour. He displays the Bhumisparsa mudra with his left hand and Santikaran mudra with his right hand (thumb and index finger being joined to form a loop).

In some instances he is also described as blue in colour. He holds a sword with his right hand and holds the banner marked with a Visvavajra in his left hand.

In Gunakarandavyuha sutra, it says that when Buddha Shakyamuni was about to give a discourse on this sutra, he sat in an ecstatic samadhi called Sarvasansodhana i.e. the purifier of everything. Golden rays of light illuminating the whole province were seen originating from some unknown region in that place. At that time Bodhisattva Sarvanivarana was also present there. He was struck by that and asked thè reason. Buddha Shakyamuni told him that Lord Avalokiteshvara was preaching for the sinners of Avici Hell and the rays, after purifying the sinners, were to come there to tame the ignorant and evil-doers. Thereafter, at the request of Bodhisattva Sarvanivama, Lord Buddha performed many other discourse sessions over the grandeur of Avalokitesi ara and his philanthropic activities, which are described in the Guna Karandavyuha sutra.

The Swayambhu legend states that Great Odiayana Acarya from Kapilavastu came to Kathmandu to pay homage to Lord Swayatnhhu. He once sat in meditation on the southern mountain with a view to obtain great eight powers (*skt. astasiddhi*). He then performed a fire puja or yajna where he sacrificed live fishes (skt. *Matsya ahuti*). Pleased with this act of sacrifice, Kamadhenu cow blessed him and predicted that he would gain eight great powers in the near future. At this Lord Avalokiteshvara in his Sukhavati heaven understood that Odiyana Acarya was performing non-virtuous action due to his ignorance in order to Stop this act he called Bodhisattva Viskambhin and told him to go to the place where Odiyana Acarya was meditating. Bodhisattva Viskambhin thus stopped him from his wrong-doing and blessed him with eight great powers. Then Great Odiayana

Acarya performed other austerities and sadhanas dedicated to Akasha yogini according to the instruction of Bodhisattva Vishkambhin. Later on Bodhisattva Vishkambhin issued a stream of light into a boulder and Odiyana Acarya continued to pay homage to this sacred boulder as the emanation of Bodhisattva Vishkambhin. This boulder exists still near Pharping and called Phanikeshar Vitaraga.

Gaganganja Bodhisattva

He is also one of the great bodhisattvas among the group of eight bodhisattvas. He is either yellow or red in colour. His symbol is a Kalpa tree.

In some instance he is described as golden yellow in colour. He holds the vajra in his left hand while the right is pointed to the sky. In Tibetan Kanjur a special sutra dedicated to this Bodhisattva is extant with the name of Gaganganjasutra.

According to the Swayambhu legend Bodhisattva Gaganganja is said to have appeared in Kathmandu valley to bless Prince Gokarna who was a great sinner indulgeing in harsh and immoral speech with his father Vrisakarna.

As a result, the king sent him into exile. The king himself could not bear the evil deeds of his son and passed away with great despair. His spirit was roaming as a ghost for the same reason. He was not able to secure a happy rebirth. Later the prince also underwent torturous experiences as though from a hell realm in exile. Upon realizing his misdeeds, he later performed an act of penance in Punya Tirtha near Gokarna. Bodhisattva Gaganganja appeared in front of prince Gokarna and instructed hint to perform the necessary death rituals and offering ceremonies in honour of his deceased father. Bodhisattva Gaganganja told him that this act would definitely be helpful in securing a good rebirth for his deceased father. Since then Nepalese people are continuing to offer pinda dana to their deceased fathers in the day of Shravan Krishna i.e. new moon day of July-August. A monument dedicated to Bodhisattva Gaganganja still exists to this date in the Gokarna area where hundreds of devotees perform Astamivrata and ritual offerings.

Bodhisattva Vajrapani

Bodhisattva Vajrapani is the embodiment of the power of Lord Buddha's compassion. He is always depicted in wrathful aspect.

Vajrapani's body is blue in colour and his hair has yellow ochre. He wears a tiger skin around his waist. He is usually depicted in two arms aspect but can be seen in four arms aspect as well.

He is a major Bodhisattva easily recognized as holding a vajra with his right hand and left hand displaying threatening vitarka mudra. His body seems to be massive and in a pose of warrior. Under his feet he controls two live snakes. He wears all sorts of bodhisattva ornaments and also a garland of snakes. He has a wide and wild roaring mouth rimmed with lacquered red lips. His eyebrows are like the flame, with his moustache and beard being curled.

Vajrapani is often depicted with Avalokiteshvara and Manjushree representing the Buddha's power of compassion (Vajrapani), the great compassion (Avalokiteshvara) and the great wisdom (Manjushree).

Vajrapani's wrathfulness, snake ornament and his pose as a warrior all serve to convey the force and vitality of the enlightened energy as it combats ignorance, greed, fear and other delusions. Vajrapani is said to be the companion Bodhisattva of Buddha Shakyamuni. While the Buddha was residing at Gridhkuta hill, the site where Lord Buddha delivered the Prajnaparamita doctrines, his jealous cousin Devadutt attempted to assassinate him. He sent a huge boulder rolling down the hill, but just as it was about to hit the Buddha, Vajrapani appeared and split the boulder into pieces so that it could fall harmlessly near Buddha.

Another story is this that a brahman called Ambattha was abusing the Buddha with many vile and impure words. He saw Vajrapani appear in the sky with his wrathful aspect. Terrified of Vajrapani, Brahman Ambattha confessed his evil deeds in front of Buddha Shakyamuni.

Manjushree Bodhisattva

Manjushree is the embodiment of the characteristics of the Enlightened Mind i.e. Discriminating Wisdom. Manjushree has the ability to see the nature of reality as it is. He is seen holding the flaming sword of wisdom with his tight hand and a book called Prajnaparamita with his left hand. He has many names such as Manjuvajra, Manjughosa, Vagishvara, Arapacana, etc. In Mahayana Buddhist tradition he is regarded as having supreme wisdom among Bodhisattvas. He is also called prince of the Dharma because of his eloquent wisdom.

According to the Surangamasamadhi sutra, he became a Buddha in past immeasurable aeons ago although he manifests as the assistant to the Shakyamuni Buddha. According to the Manjushreevyuhalamkara Sutra, he was the teacher of countless Buddhas in the past and led numerous cultivators to certify the fruit of Buddhahood. He is thus called the Mother of all Buddhas in Three worlds. In Namasangiṭi text he is designated as Adi-Buddha, the primordial Buddha i.e. embodiment of All self-existing Awareness. He is said to have cut the gorge of Chovar hill with his flaming sword Chandrahasa and let the waters flow out and thereby opened the valley for human habitation and spread the Buddha dharma.

In Gandavyuha sutra it is said that Manjushree incited Bodhisattva Sudhana to seek dharmas of enlightenment from 53 Kalyanamitras.

Wu-Tai-Shah Mountain of Mainland China is said to be the bodhimanda of Manjushree.

Maitreya Bodhisattva

Maitreya Buddha is regarded as the Buddha to be born in the future, hence the name Future Buddha, of this fortunate aeon. It is said that his birth will take place in city of Ketumati (Banares?) ruled by Cakravarti king Sankha. At that time the human beings will live for 80,000 years. It is said that Shakyamuni Buddha before leaving Tusita heaven announced that Maitreya would be his successor.

It is also said that Asanga, the renowned sage of the Mahayana, went to Tusita heaven to meet Maitreya and he was initiated into five doctrines or works viz:

1. Uttaratantra Sastra
2. Abhisamayalamkara
3. Mahayana Sutralamkara
4. Madhyanta Vibhaga Sastram
5. Dharma Dharmata Vibhaga Sastram

Maitreya as a Bodhisattva was quite popular in Theravada countries. His images can be found in Sri Lanka, Burma and Thailand. His images can also be seen in China and Tibet.

Maitreya is yellow in color. He holds in his right hand the flower of Nagakeshar and with the left the mendicant bowl. When he is represented in Buddha posture, his hands show dharmacakra mudra with his legs down on the lotus.

11

Forms of Avalokitesvara in Nepal

Padmapani Lokeshvara

Padmapani is also a form of Avalokiteshvara. He is generally seen standing at the right side of Buddha Amitabha in Sukhavati Heaven. He is depicted red in colour. He holds a lotus flower in his left hand and shows varada mudra with his right hand.

He wears an antilope skin on the shoulders. He wears all the ornaments typical of a bodhisattva symbolizing his enlightened experiences. He wears a crown and his hair is bound to form a topknot. Sometimes it is eclipsed by an effigy of Amitabha Buddha. When there is no effigy of Amitabha Buddha in the crown of Padmapani, he is then white in colour.

A legend says that once an elephant was going to pick up a lotus flower in a pond. Unfortunately he slipped into the mud. He cried in agony and prayed for Narayana. In the mean time Arya Avalokiteshvara was in that jungle and he heard the prayer. Immediately he took the form of Narayana and rescued the elephant from the marshy pond. Then Avalokiteshvara took the lotus offered by the elephant and went to Jetavana grove where Buddha Shakyamuni was residing. He in turn offered this lotus flower to Buddha Shakyamuni. Buddha Shakyamuni thanked Avalokiteshvara for his offer of the lotus flower and requested him to offer it to Lord Amitabha on his behalf. Avalokiteshvara told the whole story to Lord Amitabha Buddha.

Appreciating the philanthropic deeds of Avalokiteshvara, Buddha Amitabha told him to keep that lotus flower forever and continue the act of benefitting all sentient beings. Later on Avalokiteshvara was known as Padmapani Lokeshvara.

In Kathmandu valley numerous images of Padmapani Bodhisattva or Lokeshvara are found. Padmapani Lokeshvara found in Shreegha vihara in Kathmandu is believed to be of the fifth century of Christian era. According to Pandit Hem Raj Shakya

202 images or sculptures of Padmapani carved in stones are found in Patan city alone dating as early as the Lichchavi period.

Amoghpash Lokeshvara

Amoghpash Lokeshvara is a multi-armed form of Avalokiteshvara that seems to have been popular in Nepal since the middle ages. The name suggests that he is the Lord of the world with infallible noose, which leads suffering sentient beings to enlightenment.

According to the Amoghpasa Hrdaya Dharani Sutra, ninety-one aeons ago Avalokiteshvara received the transmission of this Dharani from Lokeshvararaja Tathagata. Since then he used that dharani to teach limitless sentient beings. As Avalokiteshvara manifests transformed body (Nirmanakaya) and uses this dharani to ferry over sentient beings he is then addressed as Amoghpasa. Amoghpasa is popular not only in Nepal but in all countries where Mahayana Buddhism has spread. The images of Amoghpasa can he found in Java, China and Japan. According to Dr. Luciano Petech, the image of Amoghpasa in its earliest form can he found in the Arya Amoghpasa Sutra preserved in Kaisar Library, Kathmandu.

Amoghpasa has one face and wears a saffron dress. He has eight hands with the right hands showing the gesture of fearlessness, the boon granting gesture, the noose and holding the string of beads while the left hands holding a trident, a scripture, a white lotus and a water pot.

He has three divine eyes looking on the triple world. His first right hand in abhayamudra symbolizes that one who practices Astami brata sincerely protects them from falling into lower realms. The second right hand displaying Varadamudra shows that those who practice and generate compassion and Bodhicitta receive all desirable objects. The third hand holding Amoghpasa or infallible noose symbolizes that he has infallible skill in means to convert ignorant sentient beings into the path of liberation. The fourth right hand holding a rosary signifies that by the recitation of the six syllable mantras of Avalokiteshvara, one frees oneself from the bondage of samsara.

Again among four left hands, one holding a water pot signifies that he has the capacity of empowering all the sentient beings into Buddhahood. The second left hand holding a lotus signifies that he frees the sentient beings residing in hell realms from the suffering of intense heat and cold just like a lotus emerges from muddy water. The third left hand holding a trident signifies that he purifies three poisons of sentient beings i.e. lust, ill will and stupidity. The fourth left hand holding a scripture signifies that he imparts wisdom to the devotees and thereby they attain liberation from cyclic existence.

Six-Syllabled Or Sadakshary Lokeshvara

Six-syllabled Avalokiteshvara is widely used for devotional practice of Yidam or Istadevata. His six-syllabled mantra *Om Mani Padme Hung* has become so popular that it has been a household mantra for every buddhist in Mahayana tradition. It is said that the fully enlightened mind has three great qualities: Great compassion, Wisdom and the Skillful Means to benefit all sentient beings. The great compassion is the attitude that all the sentient beings be freed from every form of suffering, pain and dissatisfaction. Such, great compassion and altruistic attitude, which strives toward complete enlightenment for the benefit of all sentient beings is here symbolized by this four-armed Avalokiteshvara.

The traditional author great Thangtong Gyalpo describes him thus:

Upon a white lotus and moon seat, the syllable *Hrib* arises. The letter then transforms into four-armed Avalokiteshvara. He has a white, translucent body that radiates five coloured lights. He has a smiling expression and gazes upon us with compassionate eyes. He has four hands, the first two pressed together at his heart and the lower two holding a crystal rosary and a white lotus. He is adorned with silks and jewelled ornaments and wears an upper garment of an antilope skin. His crown is adorned with Amitabha. If we rely on this sadhana of Avalokiteshvara and recite mantra *Om Mani Padme Hung* with strong faith and devotion we will definitely achieve realizations of great compassion and supreme Buddhahood. It is said that as Avalokiteshvara benefits sentient beings with the help of six-syllable mantra he is called Six-syllabled Lokeshvara. The importance and grandeur of this mantra is well explained in the Guna Karandavyuha sutra. About a half dozen images of Six-syllabled Lokeshvara are found in Patan alone in stone sculptures.

Hariharihariharivahan Lokeshvara

This is one of the most interesting sculptors/forms of Avalokiteshvara. It seems that this form of Avalokiteshvara is basically of Nepalese origin. According to Swayambhu Purana, when the great bodhisattva Manjushree drained the lake called Nagarhad (now Kathmandu valley) all the Nagarajas especially Takshaka were very angry. Bodhisattva Samantabhadra pacified them all except the Takshaka. He killed many people and animals. Due to this act of violence he was afflicted with leprosy. He repented his actions and began to pray for Arya Avalokiteshvara in order to eliminate his had karma. Due to his strong devotion to Lord Avalokitesvara he was cured of his disease.

One day while he was leisurely sun basking in a nearby river, a hungry Garuda saw him there. He alighted down and tried to devour Takshaka. Since Takshaka was the king of Nagas, he had great strength. They began to engage in a ferocious battle. He soon began to drag Garuda into river and intended to kill him. Garuda, finding himself about to be killed, invoked his protector Vishnu who came there immediately to save him. As Vishnu was about to cut off the head of Takshaka with his Sudarsanacakra i.e. whirling disc, Takshaka, realizing his upcoming defeat, prayed for Avalokiteshvara for his protection. Avalokiteshvara arrived there instantly flying over his lion vehicle. Vishnu was ashamed to find Avalokiteshvara, Lord of compassion in front of him and instantly bowed before him throwing away his Sudrashan Chakra and paid homage.

Thereafter Takshaka and Garuda too retreated from the battle and joined to the worship of Avalokiteshvara. After that Vishnu offered himself to Avalokiteshvara to be his vehicle. In the mean time, the lion also offered himself to be the vehicle of Garuda, in turn. Nagaraja Takshaka also offered to be the vehicle of the lion. Thus this composite image of Avalokiteshvara on Vishnu, and on Garuda, then on the lion, all then on Takshaka. The original image of this unique Lokeshvara is at Changu Narayan, a hill above Sodhani Tirtha, near Bhaktapur.

Harihariharivahan Lokeshvara's body is depicted white in colour. He has six arms. Out of his three right hands one hand displays the witness gesture the second hand holds a rosary and the third right hand displaying bodhyanga mudra. The three left hands hold staff, Krishnajina and a vase. He is seated on the vehicle of Naga, lion, Garuda and Narayana. His images in bronze and stones can he seen at Swayamhhu in Kathmandu, Kwabahal, and Okubahal in Patan.

Sristikanta Lokeshvara

Among the many forms of Avalokiteshvara Sristikanta Lokeshvara is the one derived from the text Gunakarandavyuha Sutra. This Sutra was basically composed in the 3rd or 4th century. This was the time Lord Maitreya transmitted the teachings of Buddha nature to Acarya Asanga (Circa 350 A.D.) The Sutra says that when this Universe was empty except Prabhasvara, there were no physical elements like earth, water, air, and fire. Adi-Buddha appeared in the first place. He meditated on a samadhi called Lokasansarjana with a view to create the Universe. First of all he emanated Aryavalokiteshvara. He in turn meditated deeply on samadhi called Lokotbhava thereby creating moon from his right eye, sun from his left eye, then the system of day and night evolved.

He then created Mahadeva from his forehead, Brahma from his shoulders, Narayana from his heart, Sarasvati from his upper and lower teeth, Vayu deva from his mouth; Varuna Nagaraja from his abdomen, Mahalaxmi from his left knee, Agnideva from his navel, Kuvera from his right knee, the earth from his sole. In this way he created many other important devas, and assigned them characteristic duties for each. These created Devas gladly accepted their duties and promised to keep them forever. They also promised to practice Bodhisattvacarya for the sake of all sentient beings. Avalokiteshvara told them that if they kept their promises and worked for the benefit of all sentient beings they would then attain Buddhahood in future.

We have already dealt with Dharmakaya or Adi-Buddha or Prabhasvara (in the Introduction) that Adi-Buddha never meant first Buddha. It must be known that Prabhasvara is rendered as Clear light. The nature of our mind is empty in essence yet it can cognize everything. This principle is constant throughout the three divisions of time. It is also known as primordially self-existing wakefulness or dharmakaya nature of our mind. This nature is inherented by all sentient beings - so they are all potential Buddhas. When one realizes that one's mind is empty and yet cognizant one realizes Buddhahood. When one's veil of obscurations are, removed one's buddha nature is manifested simultaneously. To communicate this idea the sutra describes it in a theistic sense that there appeared first a Buddha when nothing was there. Although the Sutra illustrates in a theistic sense, the inner meaning of the sutra is to communicate this Buddha nature theme.

Iconographically, Sristikanata Lokeshvara is red in colour. He holds a lotus flower with his left hand and displays varada mudra with his right hand. He is generally depicted in a standing posture with a dozen important deities emanating. His image can be seen in the Golden Window of Patan Durbar Square, Patan.

Rakta Arya Avalokiteshvara

Rakta Arya Avalokiteshvara is one of the many forms of Avalokiteshvara. According to a chronicle, Avalokiteshvara emanated himself as a son of Yaksha in Kamuni Kshetra in Assam. He was brought to Kathmandu with great effort by king Narendra Deva, Guru Bandhudatta and a farmer Lalita. In the seventh century Nepal there was a famine for twelve years. People suffered much due to drought. Following the suggestion of Acarya Bandhudutta the act of bringing a child who was the emanation of Arya Avalokiteshvara was carried out successfully. Nepalese people called this deity as Bungadeo. Every year a chariot festival is celebrated with great pomp and splendour in Patan city. All the valley citizens observe this festival with gaiety and happiness.

This deity is generally red in colour. He has four arms. He holds an arrow and goad with his right hands and bow and noose with his left hands. He stands under the Asoka tree, which has blossomed into red flowers. A bronze image of Rakta Aryavalokiteshvara is installed on the central courtyard of Hiranyavarna Mahavihara, Patan. The image of this deity is very rare. Only the human manifestation in the form of Bungadeo is popular in Kathmandu valley.

Lokanath Lokeshvara

In common parlance all the Buddhas and bodhisattvas can be called Lokanath i.e. Lord of the world but in a specific sense Lokanath is one of the forms of Avalokiteshvara. Nepalese textual sources describes him thus:

He is white in colour. He sits in the Lalita attitude. In his matted hair the figure of Vajradharma exhibiting varadamudra in the right hand and holding lotus in his left hand appears. He is said to have originated from the seed syllable *Hrih*. He exhibits varadamudra with his right hand and holds a lotus in the left. In the Lokanath mandala, he is said to be surrounded by Tara to his right and Hayagriva on the left. A host of eight bodhisattvas and others surrounds him. The image of this form of Lokeshvara is very rare. Both the Padmapani and Lokanatha hold the Lotus with their left hands and' this creates confusion in identification.

One Thousand-Armed Lokeshvara Or Sahasrabhuja Lokeshvara

This is one of the many forms of Avalokiteshvara comprising 108 as depicted in the Kanak Caitya Mahavihara of Kathmandu.

He manifests in many forms in order to help sentient beings. His 1,000-armed form is described as follows:

His body is white. He has 1,000 arms and one thousand eyes. However his original two hands and two eyes are not included. Out of 1,000 arms of Avalokiteshvara, 38 arms of this lokeshvara are depicted with various symbols or emblems, which are given below:

Right Arms	Left Arms
1. Jewel skt. *Ratna*	1. Svetamegha
2. Noose skt. *pasa*	2. Kamandalu
3. Alms bowl skt. *Pindapatra*	3. Padma
4. Sword skt. *Khadga*	4. Khadga
5. Vajrai	5. Sankha
6. Suryakantmani	6. Kapala
7. Candrakantmani	7. Akshamala
8. Dhanu	8. Ghanta

9. A root shoot of willow	9. Vajra
10. Camara	10. Amkush
11. Kavaca	11. Danda
12. Kalasa	12. Nirmita Buddha
13. Parasu	13. Devalaya
14. Akshamala	14. Pustakapothi
15. Utpala	15. Cakra
16 Kamandalu	16. Buddha pratima
17. Surya	17. Phala
18. Pundarika	18. Padmakeshara
19. Dhanyamanjary	19. Ratna

Sometimes he is depicted with emblems with eight arms only carrying rosary, disc, varada mudra and jewel with his right hands and lotus, bow, vase and clapping Ratna with his left hands. He wears antilope skin on his shoulders symbolizing compassionate nature. He wears all the bodhisattva ornaments like earrings, and so on. He has eleven heads. The eleventh one being his spritual sire Buddha Amitabha. It is said that Bodhisattva Avalokiteshvara made the commitment in front of Buddha Amitabha to intentionally manifest into the three realms of samsara in order to liberate all sentient beings from samsara and to be their supreme guide. He also vowed that if by chance his compassion and courageous mind of mercy for sentient beings were to decrease, then let his head and body just completely crack and fall into one thousand pieces. Receiving blessings from Buddha Amitabha, Avalokiteshvara went through universal manifestations into the three realms of samsara.

Thereby he went to Hell and emancipated them from both the hot and cold hells by teaching *Om mani pad me hung*. He in turn went to ghost realm, human, Asura and Deva realms to free the sentient beings from their respective suffering. He absolutely emptied the ocean of suffering. Following which he went back to Buddha Amitabha and declared that the liberation had been effected. Buddha Amitabha said to him, "you should look again, look back again and again into the world." And as he did, there he saw once again that sentient beings were in samsara and in sorrow, he became so disappointed when he saw the sight. Then his enlightened thought (Bodhicitta) decreased in the moment and he lost his courage. He became disappointed in the very presence of Buddha Amitabha.

He felt how could the time come to liberate all sentient beings forever from this type of condition. And instantly when his mind left with sorrow, his body and head just cracked and fell apart into one thousand pieces, and then he fainted.

Avalokiteshvara thus fainted, and Buddha Amitabha said to him, "My son where has your courage, your mental strength gone?" He picked up all the pieces of his body and the head. At the same time he said, "this happened because of your prayer. You deserve the praise of all Buddhas since your prayer was efficacious. However, noble son! Don't worry." Thereby he blessed his broken heads into eleven faces and he sat upon those heads and his broken body into one thousand hands like one thousand petals of the lotus. Thereafter he said, "I bow to you because your thousand hands are the hands of the thousand universal emperors and those eyes in each of the palms of the hands are the eyes of one thousand Buddhas who will appear in this fortunate aeon. After that Avalokiteshvara appeared in many different forms in order to tame the suffering sentient beings and he successfully accomplished many events.

The image of 1,000 armed Avalokiteshvara in stone is rare in Kathmandu valley. The bronze images can be seen here and there. Basically a system of fasting ceremony called Nyune from Tibet came to Kathmandu too, through Tibetan Buddhists Masters. In this fasting ceremony the practice; or sadhana is usually devoted to this form of Avalokiteshvara.

Thousand armed Avalokiteshvara form of image can be found in China too. A giant image of 1,000 armed Avalokiteshvara (ht. 360cm) is installed in the Maitreya temple in Tainan. It was carved out of wood and has aesthetical value.

12

Manjushree and his Forms and Deities in Nepal

Arapacana Manjushree

Manjushree embodies wisdom aspect of an enlightened mind. This is the ability to see into the true nature of reality of the persons and the phenomena. Manjushree has the ability to discriminate correct views of reality as it is. In order to benefit the sentient beings he too, manifests in different forms. In this form of Manjushree, he is single faced symbolizing his wisdom as non-dual. He holds the flaming sword in his right hand to symbolize cutting off the root of the delusion, which is the cause of suffering, ignorance, and of self-grasping. He holds the scriptural text entitled 'Perfection of wisdom', which cuts off all delusions. He sits in the Vajraparyanka attitude. Four companions with few exceptions always accompany him.

He is invoked especially for increasing intelligence by reciting his mantra viz.: *Om A Ra Pa Ca Na Dhih* many times.

This form of Manjushree has a special relationship with Kathmandu valley because it was he who drained the water of Kathmandu valley to make it habitable land. According to Swayambhu legend it is said that he came to Kathmandu valley with his consorts Kesini and Upakesini. His two companions are said to be Jalinikumar and Chandraprabha Kumar who were bodhisattvas. As the water receded, the sacred hill of Swayambhu Stupa appeared. This was the contribution of great bodhisattva Manjushree Arapacana.

Manjughosha

This form of Manjushree as described in Sadhanamala, is golden yellow in colour and rides on a lion. He is decked in all sorts of bodhisattva ornaments and his hands exhibit dharmacakra mudra.

He displays an utpala flower in his left hand and bears an image of Akshobhya on his crown. He is invoked by his popular mantra *Om vagisvara Muh.*

Concerning his activities in Nepal a legend is befitting to cite here. There was an Upasaka called Buddhapala in the city of Pancala. He was very learned and had many disciples who learnt many orthodox sciences under him. Unfortunately his only son called Manjugarta had not been educated. He was too dull to learn most of the sciences Buddhapala taught to his disciples. So he decided to send his son to Manjushree Caitya near Swayambhu hill to receive blessings from Manjushree. So he sent his son there along with some of his disciples with the necessary instructions. On his way to Manjushree Caitya he came to a farm where sugar cane was cultivated. Young Manjugarta was enchanted with the place. He wanted to stay there forever.

Instead of reciting *Om Na Mo Vagisvaraya* at the site of Manjushree Caitya he was busy testing and chewing succulent sugarcane. His friends suggested him if he was not interested to visit Manjushree he could recite his mantra from the same place where he was enjoying sugarcane. Accepting their proposal Manjugarta and his friends started reciting *Om Na Mo Vagisvaraya* with devotion.

Manjughosa instantly appeared in the sugarcane field with his divine form as we have described above. Even when Manjughosa appeared there this young Manjugarta was not interested to pay homage to him but through his friends suggestion he paid homage to Manjughosa. Later, Manjughosa blessed Manjugarta and predicted that he would be a master of all orthodox sciences. His ignorance was eliminated instantaneously with mere touch. Young Manjugarta later composed a hymn of praise to Manjughosa entitled 'Manjuvajra Strotram' which is still sung by the Nepalese devotees till today.

Vagisvara Manjushree or Dharmadhatu Vagisvara

Dharmadhatu Vagishvara when depicted in sculptures is eight armed, four faced, and reddish-white in colour. His right face is red, left face is yellowish-red and back face is lotus red in colour. He holds the bow and the arrow, the noose and goad, scripture and Khadga and bell and the vajra in the respective pair of hands. He sits on moon disc on a double lotus in lalita attitude. He wears all the bodhisattva ornaments and garments and bears on his crown an image of Amitabha.

Another form of Vagisvara Manjushree is single faced. He holds sword with his right hand and jewel in his left hand. He resides in the heart of Buddha Ratna Samhhava.

Different forms of Manjushree images in stone and bronze are scattered in various places. More than six-dozen images in stone are found in Patan city alone thus deserving the name Manjupattan.

Manjuvajra

Manjushree manifested in many different forms and names in order to deliver sentient beings from their ignorance. According to Swayambhu Purana he manifested himself in a human being as Manjuvajra Acarya and performed his bodhisattva deeds in the land of Swayambhu, self-born i.e. the primordial Buddha.

His human manifestation of Manjushree is deified in tantric lore as seated on the back of a lion. He is of beautiful golden colour resembling Buddha Vairocana. His three faces have yellow, blue and white colour. He is six armed. In his right hands he is holding the sword, varada mudra and the arrow and his left hands are holding scripture, blue lotus i.e. Utpal flower and the bow.

Manjushree Namasangiti

Manjushree Namasangiti is one of the important manifestations of Manjushree, the embodiment of wisdom of all the Buddhas. It is said that he was already enlightened countless aeons ago. During Shakyamuni's time he appeared himself as one of his eight chief bodhisattva disciples. Countless Buddhas of ten directions have been his disciples. Therefore he was called Adi-Buddha Manjushree. Namasangiti text has more than eight hundred words of deep spiritual significance describing this deity.

In the usual form, Namasangiti had one head and twelve arms. He is seated with dhyanamudra. He wears all the bodhisattva ornaments typical of Sambhogakaya aspects. He has Ushnisa in his head and wears a crown. His uppermost arms above his head are in the uttarabodhi mudra i.e. two hands folded to form a prostration attitude. His other two hands at the breast level are in dharmacakra or (abhaya mudra?). Two other hands are in tarpana mudra i.e. about to offer water from the alms bowl. Two hands hold an alms bowl kept in the lap. Two hands at the shoulder level hold sword and scripture on a lotus and the other two hands hold bow and arrow. This form of Namasangiti is very popular in Kathmandu valley.

TARA & HER FORMS

Green Tara

Tara represents the entire enlightened activities of all Buddhas and hence she is called the mother of the Buddhas of three times. It is said in a sutra that Avalokiteshvara Bodhisattva saved and ferried countless suffering beings over from the sea of birth and death. It happened one day when Avalokiteshvara looked at the misery of the world. He shed tears from his eyes out of great compassion. The tears turned into a lotus flower from, which appeared a white and green Tara who said to him, "Please don't be sad. We'll assist you in liberating living beings, although they are countless in number, the power of our vow is also immeasurable".

Since then they had been liberating countless numbers of living beings daily. The name of Tara was thus known to all buddhas in ten directions.

There are 21 forms of Tara (the Saviouress). In reality they are all the transformed bodies of Avalokiteshvara, the Buddha of compassion.

Green Tara appears as young beautiful maiden. Her body is green in color. She has one face and two arms she wears a crown bedecked with five buddha images. She wears all kinds of bodhisattva ornaments studded with jewels and celestial garments of varied colour. She sits on a lotus throne in Lalita attitude in half lotus posture. Her left hand shows the gesture of refuge vows and right hand the varada mudra because she is quick to answer the petitions of those who seek her aid. Tara is known as the great liberator from eight kinds of danger or fears. The cultivation of Tara sadhana will eliminate all demoniac and karmic obstacles, eradicate disaster and lengthen one's life span.

White Tara

The origin of White Tara is the same as mentioned earlier about Green Tara. She appeared out of tear drops of Avalokiteshvara when he saw that the beings in Samsara are still full of misery in spite of his efforts to liberate them. This form of Tara is described in the meditational texts as follows:

White Tara is seated in full Vajra posture and her left hand, which is poised at the heart holds the stem of a lotus that opens into a blossom beside her left shoulder. Her right hand is in the Varada mudra symbolizing supreme generosity. She is seated upright on a moon disc. She is wearing all sorts of precious ornaments and looks like a beautiful maiden of sixteen years of age. An Amitablia Buddha image sits upon the head as a crown.

The practice of white Tara is basically performed in order to prolong life as well as for healing purposes. It is said that because Arya Tara is the collective manifestation of the enlightened activity of all Buddhas, her sadhana is easily accomplished. The recitation of her Mantra merely a hundred thousand times with the motivation of Bodhicitta will cause avertion of hindrances.

Bhrikuti Tara

The concept of Bhrikuti Tara is noted in the earliest text of Arya Manjusreemulakalpa. She appears along with Arya Tara and a host of other feminine divinities called Vidyarajnis in named Mandalavidhana Parivarta of that sutra. Bhrikuti is also mentioned in Hevajra tantra. She is generally depicted as a companion deity of some forms of Avalokiteshvara viz. Khasarpana, Padmanarteshvara, Amoghpasa, etc. Bhrikuti appears in different forms. When she appears in blue colour, she is depicted as three headed and a six armed form. When yellow she is single faced three eyed and four armed and with frowning eyebrows. Her four hands hold a rosary, a trident, a Kalasa and display varada mudra.

Taranatha in his history of Buddhism in India describes a visit of an upasaka Santivarman from Pundravardhana to the top of the Potala hill, the abode of Avalokiteshvara. It is said that Santivarman once prayed to Bhrikuti to cross a sea and there appeared a girl with a raft and who took him across.

While climbing Potala hill, an upasaka saw an image of Bhrikuṭi on the way up the hill. It is also said that Bhrikuti Tara manifested herself as a Nepalese princess in seventh century, who was married to the Tibetan king, Srong btsan sGampo (617-650 A.D.). Bhriku.i Devi was instrumental in diffusing Buddhism in Tibet. She brought the artistic images of Arya Tara, Avalokiteshvara and Akshobhya Buddha into Tibet.

Vasudhara

Vasudhara is one of the important and popular feminine deities in Nepalese Buddhist society. Vasudhara Vrata, which is performed to honour this deity for two consecutive days once a year, is very popular event among Nepalese Buddhists. She is believed to be the bestower of wealth and prosperity similar to Laxmi Devi in Hinduism. It is said that through the practice of Vasudhara Vrata devotees accumulate seven kinds of prosperity i.e. wealth, quality, offspring, long life, happiness, praise and wisdom. She is described in the meditational texts as follows:

She has three faces and six arms. She is seated in Lalita attitude. Her right foot is rested on a conch placed over a vase with a lotus. Her three right hands hold a rosary, jewels, displaying of varada mudra and feet three hands bold a vase, dhanyam anjary (rice stalk) and a scripture. She wears all the precious ornaments and silk garments. She appears as a young girl of sixteen years of age. She is golden yellow in colour. She has an image of Buddha Ratna Sambhava on her crown.

The reddish white, yellow and dark red faces of the deity symbolize three eras of the Universe i.e. creation, existence and destruction. Her Varada mudra symbolizes that she bestows seven kinds of prosperity to all sentient beings especially the multiplicity of offspring. The jewel symbolizes that one's wishes are fulfilled the rosary symbolizes that through repeated investigation of our natural state or reality one's wisdom and qualities will be developed. The auspicious vase symbolizes that she confers the initiation on devotees, who thus attain high status or increase of praise or fame. The second left hand holding dhanyamanjary symbolizes that through the power of food grains one's life is sustained or life span increased. The third left hand holding scripture symbolizes that one gains insight of emptiness or increase in wisdom.

Kurukulla

There are many forms of the deity Kurukulla. But the most important form is called Tarodbava Kurukulla. She is red in colour with red garments, red ornaments and seated on a red lotus. She has four arms. Two left hands show her charging a flowery arrow on a flowery bow ready to strike and other two hands hold a noose and a goad. She appears as beautiful maiden in a dancing posture and displays lovely sentiments. The deity Kurukulla is said to confer success on devotees particularly in the tantric ritual of subjugating, enchanting men, women, ministers and the kings.

Prajnas Of Five Buddhas (Panca Buddhas)

The earliest tantra dealing with the Prajnas of Five Tathagatas is the Guhyasamaja. According to Benoytosh Bhattacharya this tantra dates back as old as the third century A.D. Another treatise which deals with these Buddha Prajnas is Pancakara of Advayavajra (11th century A.D.). A recent study of Prof. Mallar Ghosh has thrown a great light on the historical development of the usage of these deities. Modern scholars often use the term Buddha Sakti for these five deities viz. Locana, Mamaki, Pandara, Tara and Vajradhatveshvary. But the use of the term sakti does not conform with the Buddhist conception. The term Sakti, which is used to symbolize energy, action or power, is associated only with some forms of Hindu deities. In Buddhist tantras these deities symbolize the essence or prajnarupa or svabhava of five Buddhas. It is strange to note that not a single sadhana is devoted to these live Prajnas. They appear only in Yab-yum position and they are not given any active function.

The images of these deities are very rare. However a fine specimen of these five Prajnas can be found in the Swayambhu Caitya with the exception of Vajradhatveshvary.

Locana

In the Pancakara of Advayavajra Samgraha, she is said to be originated from the seed syllable *Lom,* white in complexion. She belongs to Tathagata kula. Her recognition symbol is a wheel. She is said to be Prajna of Vairocana. She is said to be similar in nature as Lord Vairocana. She is seated in Lalita asana and displays Varadamudra with her right hand. Her left palm is on the chest. from both the palms rise the stalks of lotus, supporting a Vajra.

In Hevajra Tantra and its commentary it is said that Locana, Mamaki, Pandara and Tara represent the four elements i.e. earth, water, fire and air. She has many forms, some peaceful and some wrathful. She can be found in two armed, six armed and eight armed as described in various mandalas. Her images are very rare. A magnificent image of Locana can be found in the Swayambhu Stupa. In the Gurumandala rite of Nepalese Buddhists Vajracharyas make offerings to the five Buddhas and their Prajnas.

The special characteristic of this deity is that those devotees engrossed in delusion acquire all pervasive wisdom through the sadhana of Buddha Vairocana and Locana. It is said that the essence of delusion is also dharmakaya, which is free from thought constructs. So through the practice, delusion is transmuted into wisdom of all pervasive awareness. (*skt. Suvisuddha dharmadhatu jnana*).

Mamaki

Mamaki is another important deity who is said to be originated from seed syllable, *Mam*. She is blue in colour. She is the embodiment of the water element. She belongs to vajra family and is the nature of hatred. Her recognition symbol is Vajra. She is the consort or Prajna of Buddha Akshobhya. Her another name is a Dvesarati.

She resides in the southwest corner. She too has many forms. She can he found in two armed, six armed, eight armed and twelve armed forms. In two-armed form she is depicted holding a vajra with her tight and her left hand resting on her thigh. In another case she is seen displaying varada mudra with her right hand and the stalk of an utpala with her left.

According to Tantric Buddhist symbolism of Newar Buddhist tradition there is a special ritual worship of Mamaki in the form of triad ritual objects (Newari: Anti, Khayakori and Thapin). The Newari word Anti is a special jar used for keeping fermented wine, Khayakori for Yoghurt and Thapin for keeping fermented beer.

Pandara

Pandara is said to be the Prajna of Amitabha Buddha. She is the same in essence with Buddha Amitabha. She is the embodiment of the fire element and is thus red in colour. She is also the embodiment of passion or lust; when transmuted it becomes wisdom of discriminating awareness.

In Vajrayana Buddhism unlike in lower vehicle it uses lust as a path to enlightenment. Whereas in lower vehicle i.e. Shravaka vehicle one refrains being lustful and practices renunciation of all sorts of wordly desires and physical pleasures.

In Pancakara of Advayavajra Samgraha, she is said to be originated from the seed syllable *Pam*. She is called Ragarati. Her recognition symbol is the lotus held in one of her hands. The guru mandala rite of Nepalese Buddhists make frequent mention of five Buddhas and their Prajnas and Nepalese Vajracharyas worship them frequently.

Tara

Tara is said to be the Prajna of Buddha Amoghsiddhi. She is the embodiment of the air element and is thus green in colour. She is also called Irsyarati i.e. the nature of jealosy. When the defilement jealosy is transmuted it becomes all accomplishing wisdom (*skt. Krityanusthan Jnana*).

In Advayavajra Samgraha, she is said to be originated from the seed syllable *Tam* of golden green colour. Her recognition symbol is a green night lotus (*skt. Utpala*). She belongs to Karma family.

She represents the enlightened activity of all Buddhas of three times. She too has many forms i.e. two armed, six armed and eight armed.

Vajradhatveshvari

She is said to be the consort of Buddha Ratna Sambhava. She is the same in essence as Buddha Ratna Sambhava. She is the embodiment of emptiness or the space element. She is yellow in colour. She is surrounded by the four Prajnas i.e.: Locana, Mamaki, Pandara and Tara.

Vajradhatveshvari as described in the Pancakara of Advayavajra Samgraha resembles Tathagata Vajrasattva. She has various forms: two armed, six armed and eight armed. Her two-arm form is described as follows:

She is seated in Lalita asana. In her right hand she displays varada mudra with the stalk of a lotus supporting a jewel and in her left hand she displays a vitarka mudra with the stalk of a lulus supporting a jewel.

Because of her role as the embodiment of Tathata or Prajnaparamita she is also called Nairatma, Vajravarahi and Jnanadakini. In Sadhanamala she is identified with six headed and twelve armed Marici whose lord is Vairocana.

DEITIES OF ANUTTARA YOGA TANTRAS

Kalacakra

Kalacakra is the deity of Highest Yoga Tantra class. Its initiation is given only to selected disciples who are qualified and have a foundation experience of renunciation, Bodhicitta and correct view of Emptiness. In Nepalese tradition too the initiation of Kalacakra is performed very often by learned Vajracharya priests. Receiving empowerment of this deity is a rare event these days.

It is said that one year after Shakyamuni Buddha attained Enlightenment, he was requested by King Candrabhadra of Shambhala to teach the Kalacakra Tantra. The Buddha then manifested himself in the form of Kalacakra meditational deity in South India and gave the full teachings and initiation of his tantra.

Kalacakra teaching was then transmitted through a line-age of seven kings and 25 propagators. The Kalacakra initiation sessions have been performed several times by His Holiness the fourteenth Dalai Lama at the present time also. Those who have received this initiation may use this meditational deity for Yidam practice.

Kalacakra has four faces, twenty-four arms and two legs. His front face is blue with bare fangs; right face is red; left white and rear yellow each with three eyes. His blue face expresses wrathfulness. The deity is adorned with many jewel ornaments, such as the earrings, the necklace, the crown, the bangles and anklets and so on. He is dressed in a tiger skin.

Among his 24 arms, 12 arms are on either side. The first four arms black, the middle red, and the last four arms are white. The first of the black arms embraces the consort and holds a vajra in the hand, the second a sword, the third a trident, and the fourth a cleaver. The first of the right red hands holds an arrow, the second a long handled vajra hook, the third a damaru, and the fourth a hammer. Again, the first of the right white hands holds a wheel, the second a sword, the third a stick, the fourth an axe. The first of the left black hands holds a bell, the second a shield, the third a khatvang, the fourth the kapala i.e. skull cup. The first of the left right hands holds a bow, the second a lasso, the third a precious Jewel, and the fourth a white lotus. The first of the left white hands holds a white conch, the second a mirror, the third an iron chain, and the fourth the head of the deity Brahma, held by the hair.

The Kalacakra has only two legs. The right one is red and left one is white symbolizing the right energy channels containing blood and left energy channels containing white Bodhicitta. The consort of Kalacakra is called Visvamati. She is yellow in colour and has four faces each with three eyes. The other three faces are white, black and red. She has eight arms, four each on the either side. The first right hand embraces Kalacakra, the second a vajra hook, the third a damaru, and the fourth a rosary. The first of her left hands embraces Kalacakra and holds a kapala filled with blood, the second hand holds a lasso, the third a lotus, the fourth a precious jewel. The consort wears a crown and is adorned with five types of ornaments. She is in union with the deity Kalacakra.

Hayagriva

Hayagriva is one of the emanations of Bodhisattva Avalokiteshvara He is also regarded as Yidam or Istadevata. He has many forms often with three faces, six arms and four legs and sometimes with huge wings. He can be recognized by a small horse head surmounted on the top of his main terrific head. The horse head neighs very loudly and it is noted that the sound is said to pierce all the false appearance of inherent existence or substantial reality.

The Hayagriva's terrific appearance is directed towards ego grasping and outer obstructions. His wrathfulness is said to be fierce compassion directed towards a self-cherishing attitude.

According to Sadhanamala, Hayagriva is red in colour. He is awesome and terrible in appearance with bare fangs. He has three eyes and brown beard. He wears a garland of skulls with teeth and lips. He is crowned with his Jata and a figure of Amitabha. His second face is that of a horse, which is blue in colour and neighs continuously. He tramples on the top of the world. He wears the snake ornaments. He is short and dwarfish and is clad in tiger skin. He threatens all the deities and asuras and holds the Vajra and staff in his two hands.

Yogambara

Yogambara is one of the most popular Yidam deities of Nepalese Buddhists. He sits on Ardhaparyanka on the moon on a double lotus placed on a lion. He is blue in colour and is three faced. His principal face is blue, the right white and the left red. He is six armed, and carries the vajra and bell with his two principal hands. He embraces his prajna Jnandakini who is also blue in colour and is bedecked with snake ornaments. In the remaining two hands he holds the breast and the arrow and in the two hands in the left he holds the lotus bowl and bow.

According to the legend, it is said that the deity Yogambara and consort Jnanadakini manifested themselves in the form of Yaksha and Yakshani in Kamarupa in Assam and gave birth to their son Lord Karunamaya whose chariot festival is continuing even today in Patan city. It is said that during the bathing ceremony of

Karunamaya, Juanadakini his mother in Yaksha form, used to come to Lagankhel in Patan and observe the ceremony residing on a tree.

Cakrasamvara

Cakrasamvara is the deity of Highest Yoga Tantra. He is one of the most popular forms of Yidam deity among Nepalese Buddhists Almost all the Shakyas and the Vajracharyas of Patan and Kathmandu regard Cakrasamvara as their tutelary deity or Yidam deity Nepalese Buddhist Vajracharyas have the age old tradition of practice of Cakrasamvara, a highly developed technique of contemplation to realize Clear light and emptiness aspect of the mind. A special tantra called Cakrasamvaramula tantra is dedicated to this Yidam deity. He has many forms. One of the popular from is described below:

Cakrasamvara in this form is deep blue in colour. He has four faces. The front face is blue-black; right face is white; back face is yellow; his left face is red. He is in ecstatic union with his consort Vajravarahi, red in colour. His front hands embrace his consorts with vajra and bell. His next right hands hold a damaru, a kattri, a trident and an axe. His next left hand holds a Khatvanga staff a severed head of Brahma, a kapala and a lasso. With his back two hands he is lifting freshly flayed skin of an elephant. He wears a crown of skulls and a garland of fifty freshly severed heads and skulls. He also wears a tiger skin loin cloth. His front face with three eyes gazes at his consort.

His consort Vajravarahi is beautiful and bright red in colour. Her hair is black. She wears bracelets and anklets as well as ornaments in her girdle. Her right arm is thrown upward holding a Kartri and her left arms circled tightly around Samvara's neck with her face posed upwards. Under her feet are the Samvara's own emanations viz. red, four-armed Kalaratri and blue four-armed Bhairava.

Both the deities Samvara and Vajravarahi are Buddhas by their own right. Their union symbolizes that wisdom and compassion are indivisible in the enlightened state. The twelve arms of Samvara symbolize twelve links of dependent origination. His garland of fresh severed heads symbolize his victory over ego grasping and self cherishing attitudes.

Hevajra

Hevajra is also one of the popular Yidam deity of Nepalese Buddhism belonging to Highest Yoga Tantra. In Hevajra Tantra, Hevajra is defined as thus:

He symbolizes Great compassion and Vajra symbolizes Wisdom (prajna). Within the composite name of Hevajra the essence of wisdom and compassion is contained in its entirety. In the Hevajra Tantra his form is described thus:

He is dark blue with a radiant aura. He has red eyes and yellow hair coiled and knotted at the top of his head. He is adorned with Pancamudra i.e. the circlet, the earrings, the necklace, the wrist, bracelets and the girdle. These five ornaments symbolize the purified aspects of five delusions. He appears wrathful and wears a tiger skin. He holds a skull in his left hand and a khatvanga rests in the crook of his left shoulder. He holds a black vajra in his right hand. He originates from the seed syllable *Hum*.

In his four arms form, he holds a human skull filled with the blood of, the devas and asuras with his left hand and a vajra in his right hand. His remaining two hands embrace his consort Vajravarahi.

In his six-armed form, he has three faces red, blue and white. His six arms symbolize the six perfections. He holds a vajra and a knife with his two right hands and a trident and a bell in his two left hands. The remaining two hands embrace his consort Vajrasrinkhala holding a kartri and a kapala. He tramples a corpse, which represents the three realms.

It is said that the practice of Hevajra and his consort is not to be disclosed to the others who have not received the empowerment. If the sadhaka does not conceal the practice it causes misfortune from snakes, fire, thieves, elementals and earth spirits.

DAKINIS

Vajrayogini

Vajrayogini is a class of deities called Dakini in Highest Yoga Tantra. She is also called Naro-Dakini. She is a celestial female Buddha form who mainfested herself in an initiatory vision to the great Pandit Mahasiddha Naropa (956-1040). She is also called Sarva buddha dakini. Dakinis can be human, or non-human who can traverse through air. She posess supernatural wisdom and power and can assist the practitioner of Vajrayana in eliminating obstacles and obstruction to their practice. She can even confer great siddhi of liberation and omniscience.

She holds a Kartri in her right hand and a skull bowl in her left. She carries a garland of severed heads and tramples upon her own emanations Bhairaba and Kalaratri beneath her feet. She holds a Khatvanga at the crook of her elbow parallel to her body position. She is almost naked but wears various ornaments.

In Kathmandu valley several temples dedicated to Vajrayogini are found. They are power centers of Nepalese Vajrayana tradition. She is said to be the on sort of Heruka Cakrasamvara.

Vajravarahi

Vajravarahi is another dakini associated with Heruka Cakrasamvara. Her status is not different from Vajrayogini. She is said to be the consort or the Prajna of Herukacakrasamvara. She is always depicted nude.

She is red in colour and stands on a reclining body of Bhairaba in dancing posture. She holds a Kartri in her right Hand on level of head and holds a kapala filled with blood in her left. She carries a khatvanga staff surmounted by three skulls. She wears a garland of fifty severed heads and various gold ornaments.

A special shrine is dedicated to Vajravarahi in Patan. For the practice of Sadhana of Vajravarahi an initiation (*skt. diksha*) is required. One of the peculiar features of this deity is that she has an excrescence near the right ear, which resembles the face of a sow hence her name Vajravarahi. Her worship is very popular in Nepal. There are numerous Caryagita dedicated to her.

Five Protectress Deities: Pancaraksha Devi

Out of so many female divinities five protectress deities, popularly called Pancaraksha are the most popular deities in the Nepalese pantheon. These deities are not so common in the Tibetan tradition. The order of these five deities is given as follows: Mahapratisara, Mahasahasra pramardani, Mahamayuri, Mahasitavati, and Mahamantranusarini. The characteristic feature of each deity is that Mahapratisara protects against sin, illness and other dangers. Mahasahasra pramardani protects against evil spirits. Mahamayuri protects against the venomous snakes and cobras, wild animals and poisonous insects. And Mahamantranusarini protects against illness.

Mahapratisara

Mahapratisara has four heads and eight arms. She is white in colour and her heads are successively yellow, white, red and green. She is seated on a lotus throne in vajraparyanka posture. She wears the diadem. In her right hands she holds a vajra, an arrow, a sword and in her left hands holds a trident, a bow and an axe while her two principal hands hold a wheel and a garment.

The recitation and sadhana of this protectress deity confer great benefit and protection. One such example befitting to this context is described in the first chapter of the Pancaraksha sutra. It is said that one who holds the dharani of Mahapratisara will be protected from all forms of illness, eliminate the past non-virtuous karma, protect from all sorts of dangers. They take rebirth in higher realms. Their body becomes a vajra body not affected by fire, weapons and others.

In Bhadrakalpavadana it is said that Buddha Shakyamuni renounced his palace life before the birth of his son Rahula. He touched his wife Yasodhara's navel with his thumb finger of right foot and made a great vow that she be protected from great dangers which were to come to her in the future. After his great renunciation Yashodhara bore his child for six years inside her womb. Before the delivery of the child Rahula his cousin Devadutta put her to many hazardous trials and tribulations. But in all cases Yashodhara came out unhurt due to the miraculous power of Mahapratisara Devi. Nepalese Buddhists thus wear amulets for their protection against various sorts of unseen dangers. These amulets contain the dharani of Mahapratisara Devi.

Mahasahasra Pramardani

Mahasahasra Pramardani has four heads and is awesome in appearance. The heads are successively white, blue, red and yellow. The deity wears a crown of human skulls and has tiger skin around her waist. The hair is dishevelled. She has eight arms. Her four right hands exhibit varadamudra, a sword, an arrow and a goad while her left hands hold a lotus, noose, bow and axe. She is seated in Lalitasana. She also wears a garland of severed human heads. She tramples upon a human corpse and is seated on a lotus throne. In Nispannayogavali she is described as having ten arms.

The characteristic feature of this protectress deity is that it protects us from evil and harmful spirits. It once happened that in the city of Vaishali a great disaster occured, lightning flashed violently, the earth trembled, many people suffered due to accidental diseases, deaths and other disastrous events. Lord Buddha through his Buddha eye saw many evil spirits giving troubles to people in the area by various means. Upon the request of four great kings the Buddha delivered the dharani of Arya Sahasrapramardani at Gridhkuta hill near Rajgir to pacify the evils caused by evil spirits. It is said that when the Buddha uttered the dharani of this deity hundreds of thousands of evil spirits ran away out of fear. For the benefit of the people of Vaishali the Buddha decided to enter their city. While entering into their city the people welcomed him with their best possible means. Then the Buddha out of compassion for all sentient beings taught the dharma which is auspicious in the beginning, in the middle and at the end. Many devas promised to protect the people who hold this dharani.

Mahamayuri

Mahamayuri has three heads. She is green in colour and her three faces are green, white and blue in colour. She is eight armed. One of her four right hands displays varadamudra while the other three hands hold a sword, vajra and jewel. In her four left hands she holds pindapatra, a jar showering jewels, a bell and a flower. She is seated on a lotus throne. She wears all the ornaments and celestial garments peculiar to a Bodhisattva.

According to the Mahamayuri sutra of Pancaraksha, there was a bhiksu called venerable Svati. He was newly ordained in the

Buddhist community of monks. He was unfortunately bitten by a poisonous snake and fainted. On seeing his condition venerable Ananda reported this incident to Buddha Shakyamuni. Lord Buddha, out of compassion for the newly ordained monk and the future ones, disclosed a dharani, which was capable of eliminating poisonous harm and malignant diseases. This was the dharani of Arya Mahamayuri.

There is another story about this deity. There was a golden King peacock in the Himalayan Mountain who used to recite Mahamayuri dharani with great devotion. It so happened one day that this king went along with his family to travel in the mountain forgetting to recite the dharani that day. Hunters caught him. Thinking of his forgetfulness of the dharani he immediately began to recite and was able to free himself. The Buddha told Ananda that the peacock king called Suvarnavabhasa (i.e. golden colored one) was none other than Buddha Shakyamuni himself. Thus this dharani is believed to be efficacious in all cases of dangers as well as for relieving poisonous harms.

Mahasitavati

According to Sadhanamala she is six armed and has three faces. She is green in colour. In her right hands she holds a lotus with the gesture of fearlessness, the arrow, the sword and in her left hands she holds a jewel banner, a bow and a lasso or a noose. She is seated in the ardhaparyanka posture and wears a crown. She wears all the ornaments of a bodisattva and sits on a lotus throne.

The characteristic feature of this deity is that she protects the beings from the evil effects of the planets, wild animals and poisonous insects.

According to the Mahasitavati Sutra, at one time Lord Buddha was dwelling at the cemetery of Sitavan in Rajagriha. At that time Venerable Rahula was troubled by many evil beings. Then Rahula went to see Lord Buddha and reported this incident with tears in his eyes. The Buddha then suggested to him to recite the dharani of Arya Sitavati for protection from all sorts of harmful influences from the evil deities, planets yakshas, snakes, non-human beings, and others. It is said that the recitation of this dharani relieves all disasters and is protected by all powerful four great divine kings.

Mahamantranusarini

Maharnantranusarini has three heads. She is green in colour. The heads are successively white, green and red. She has ten arms. With her two right hands she displays varada mudra and abhaya mudra while the other hands hold an arrow and a vajra. Two principal hands display vitarka mudra and the other two hands hold alms bowl. In her left hands she holds a bow, a jewel, a vase and a lasso. She wears a crown and is seated on a lotus throne. She wears all sorts of bodhisattva ornaments and garments appropriate for the Sambhogakaya aspect.

The characteristic feature of this deity is that she protects from illness of all types. The recitation of this dharani brings auspiciousness (*skt. Svasti*) to our family, society, country and the whole world. It drives away all the evil forces of non-human beings, asuras, ghosts, yakshas and brings peace and happiness through the power of truth contained in the Buddha's teachings.

According to the Mahamahtranusarini sutra, Lord Buddha disclosed this dharani to Venerable Ananda in the city of Rajagriha. Lord Buddha instructed Ananda to recite this dharani to the people of Vaisali where they were having disastrous events. Later the Buddha himself visited the city of Vaisali and uttered the dharani of Mahamantranusarini thereby pacifying all the calamities. Nepalese Buddhists recite this dharani sutra of auspiciousness during the marriage ceremony, ordination and other auspicious occasions or ceremonies.

Ten Wrathful Deities of Direction

In Vajrayana Buddhism the deities are classified as peaceful and wrathful. The wrathfulness is indicated toward ego grasping which is root obstruction to liberation. So the function of these deities is to remove or eliminate all sorts of obstacles or obstruction for the protection of dharma. These wrathful deities have multiple heads, arms, varying colours, forms, headdresses, instruments and the other things. It is believed that the four cardinal directions, four corners and the top and bottom quarters numbering ten have each one deity who guards and protects. The origin of these ten deities of direction is described in the first chapter of the Guhyasamaja Tantra.

In most of the tantric practices of Nepalese Vajrayana Buddhism, the offering and the worship are made to these deities with special rites performed mostly in night times. One such instance is the rite of Initiation of Cakrasamvara in its fourteen aspects. Here Vajracharyas perform the worship of these wrathful deities at the cemetery to clear away the obstacles for the practice of Cakrasamvara. They are invoked to support the practices of these sadhanas and gain realization of Mahamudra.

Yamantaka

Yamantaka presides over the eastern direction and is one of the popular deities of the Nepalese Buddhist Pantheon. It is said that he is the emanation of Bodhisattva Manjushree. With great awesome and virtuous strength, he is capable of subduing poisonous serpents and eliminating countless obstacles.

Bodhisattva Manjushree took this wrathful form in order to subdue the Lord of death. So Yamantaka symbolizes the victory of wisdom over death, evil and suffering. How Yamantaka subdued Yama, Lord of death is described in a legend. It is said that a Bonpo ascetic was just attaining the final stage of his meditative experience after a long years of samadhi. In the mean time a gang of robbers entered his cave in order to slaughter a bull they had stolen. Having cut off the bull's head they happened to see him and immediately began to attack him. This ascetic begged for mercy but they did not hear his request. They severed his head. All of sudden this severed head took the form of Yama and fitted the bull's head on to the place of his own lost head and then massacred the robbers and drank their blood from cups made of their skulls. Out of the great rage he even threatened to destroy the whole of Tibet. Then the Tibetans prayed to their protector Manjushree who then transformed himself into a wrathful appearance of Yamantaka in order to conquer Yama. In the ferocious battle that followed, Yama was subdued. He later determined to become a protector of dharma (thus the name Dharmaraja for Yama).

Among the many forms of Yamantaka, Yamantaka Vajrahhairava is the most popular. He is described in the meditational texts as follows:

Yamantaka Vajrabhairava has eight heads. The principle head is that of a bull or a buffalo. He has 34 arms and 16 feet to subdue Yama from escaping. On the top of the eight heads lies the gentle face of golden coloured image of Manjushree. His two principal hands hold a skull bowl and a vajra chopper (*skt. kartri*). The legs are clustered together. His erect phallus has bright red tip. He wears a garland of severed heads, a crown of five skulls symbolizing he has the wisdom of five Buddhas. Beneath the feet lie the subjugated deities and animals. He is usually depicted with his Prajna.

Vighnantaka

Vighnantaka presides over the northern direction and is one of the most popular wrathful deities in the Nepalese pantheon. He has different forms too. In his two arm form he stands in the Pratyalidha attitude, one face being blue in colour. He carries the Tarjanipasa in his left hand and vajra in his right hand. His appearance is ferocious, his brown hair rises straight upwards.

In his six arm form he carries a Kartri and a kapala with his two principal hands and a Damaru and a goad in his right hands with a noose and a trident in the left hand. He is green in colour. He has three faces showing green, white and red colour. His two principal hands hold his prajna as usual. In some figures lord Vighnantaka is seen trampling heavily on Ganesa, Lord of obstacles. How Lord Vighnantaka subdued Ganesh is narrated in Swayambhu legend as follows.

Once Odiyana Acarya, a great Pandita, after receiving his eight great powers (*skt. Astasiddhi*) came to Kachchapal mountains near Chovar in order to meditate. He sat on the hide of an elephant and invoked all the deities (33 crores) with the exception of Ganesh, who resides in the nearby mountain. Ganesh was surprised to see a multitude of divinities gathering there near his residence. On investigation he found that. Odiyana Acarya was practicing austerities inviting all the deities. On knowing this he was furious and ordered his retinue consisting of Putans, Kataputans, asuras, aquatic animals and others to create obstacles in his austerities. The attack of Ganesh's retinue was quite effective. Odiyana Acarya felt quite helpless and hence invoked Lord Vighnantaka, the great destroyer of obstacles. Lord Vighnantaka instantly appeared in his terrific six-armed form and vanquished the army of Ganesh and his retinue. After subduing Ganesh he instructed Odiyana Acarya that, he should perform the offering first to Ganesh the king of obstacles, in order to be successful in any effort. Thus Nepalese people started offering to Ganesh in the first place before observing any auspicious occasions, any social or religious rituals or business enterprise, in order to ensure success.

Acala

Acala is one of the wrathful deities of the direction in the northeast corner. He is blue in colour and has three faces blue, white and red. He holds a vajra and a jewel and a lotus. His two principal hands hold his Prajna in embrace. In the Nepalese Vajrayana Buddhist tradition an initiation of Acala alias Candamaharosana is essential for becoming a Buddhist priest. In Sadhanamala he is described as having one face, two arms and is squint-eyed. He looks ferocious with fangs. He wears a jewelled crown and a garland of severed heads. He carries a sword in his right hand and a noose in the left. His sacred thread is of white snake. He is clad in tiger skin and bears an effigy of Akshobhya on his crown. This Protector deity is always depicted in father-mother aspect and is never to be displayed in public.

A special tantra dedicated to Acala can be found in original Sanskrit text. His sadhana is to be performed always in secret and is to be practiced only by those who are initiated.

It is said that through his sadhana and worship, Acala will help the practitioner to eliminate disaster of drought, flood and to subdue thieves and enemies.

Mahabala

This deity Mahabala has three faces of blue, white and red colours, six arms and resides in the northwest corner. He holds a trident, a sword, a jewel and a lotus. He holds his Prajna with his two principal hands as usual.

According to Sadhanamala, he is one faced, four armed and red in colour. He looks ferocious and his brown hair rises straight upwards and is tied by a snake. He carries in his right hands; a white staff and a chowrie while the two left hands display the namaskar mudra and a raised index finger. He is clad in tiger skin, wears ornaments of snakes and stands in the Pratyalidha attitude. He bears the effigy of Amitabha on the crown.

The images of Mahabala are rare in Nepal, India and Tibet but they are found in Chinese collections. However miniature paintings of this deity are found here and there in Nepalese Buddhist monasteries. These deities are worshipped in the group of ten during initiation ceremony of Cakrasamvara.

Prajnantaka

The Protector Prajnantaka presides over the southern direction. He is white in colour. He has three faces of white, blue and red colour. He has four arms. He holds a white staff with vajra mark; a sword, a jewel and a lotus. His two principal hands embrace his prajna.

Buddhist Vajracharyas during an initiation rite have these images of ten deities painted on a wooden planks. The stone and bronze images are very rare and are available only in China.

Padmantaka

The Protector Padmaritaka presides over the western direction. He is red in colour. His three faces are of red, blue and white colours. He holds a red lotus, a sword, a jewel and a discus. His two principal hands hold his Prajna in embrace.

His images are very rare here in Nepal. But they can however be found in miniature paintings only.

Takkiraja Or Vajrayaksha

The Protector Takkiraja is the guardian deity in the southeast corner. He is blue in colour, his three faces are blue, white and red in colour. He holds a blue staff, a sword, a jewel and a lotus.

The name of Protector Takkiraja is mentioned in several strotras or hymns such as Mangalastava, which is frequently recited by Nepalese Buddhists. In this stava the devotees make great petition to these deities to remove obstacles in the ten directions and aspire for peace and happiness. In Vajrahumkara mandala he is

Vajrayaksha. He has six arms. His two principal hands hold a pestle, an arrow and a sword. His left three hands hold a bell, a bow and a wheel.

As a legend goes, if one practices the sadhana of Vajrayaksha or Takkiraja then it eliminates disasters, subdues demons and ghosts. In Japanese Buddhist circles, it is believed that if one recites his mantra for seven times before eating, the eater can escape the danger of food poisoning.

Niladanda

The Protector Niladanda presides over the southwest corner.

He has three faces showing blue, white and red colour. He has six arms. He holds a blue staff, a sword, a jewel and a lotus. His two principal hands hold prajna in embrace. As stated earlier his name is also mentioned in several stavas or hymns, which are often recited by Nepalese Buddhists. The images of Niladanda are very rare in Nepal and are mainly found in China.

Usnisa

The protector Usnisa presides over the upper direction i.e. the zenith. He is also known as Usnisacakravarti. He is yellow in colour. His three faces show yellow, blue and red colours. He holds a yellow discus, a sword, a jewel and a lotus. His two principal hands hold his prajna. His images are extremely rare in Nepal and are found only in China.

Sumbharaja

The Projector Sumbharaja presides over the nether world. He is blue in colour. His three faces are blue, white and red in colour. He holds a vajra, a sword, a jewel and a lotus. His two principal hands embrace his prajna. He is wrathful in appearance. His images are also extremely rare in Nepal.

Four Great Kings (Caturmaharajas)

Dhritarastra

Dhritarastra is one of the four Great kings in the first heaven of this desire realm. He serves as the guardian in the East. He protects the land and living beings so he is called Heavenly Lord of maintaining the country (*skt. Dhritarastra*).

He is the lord of Gandharvas. He has 91 sons ready to protect the disciples of Lord Buddha. According to the Mahasanghata Sutra, Buddha Shakyamuni told Dhritarastra to protect the Buddha dharma in the four continents of Jambudvipa with utmost care. Following his instruction Dhritarastra promised to lead all retinues of Buddhist disciples to the east of Jambudvipa so that the true dharma might he diffused in the world forever. He lives in the city of Superior sage, magnificent and situated in the east of Sumeru mountains.

According to the Dharani Sutra, this king wears various kinds of celestial robes. He holds a vina with both his hands. Nepalese Buddhists generally know him by the name of Vinaraj and his image is seen in the east corner of the roof. He is depicted as white.

Virudhak

Virudhak is yet another great king of the southern direction. He resides in the middle of Sumeru mountains. He rules over a city called Sudarsana located to the south of Sumeru Mountain. The city is extremely beautiful and occupies an area of 6,000 square yojansas. Virudhaka leads an assembly of Kumbhandas to serve as the guardian of the Buddha dharma in the southern direction.

In the past Buddha Shakyamuni instructed Virudhaka that he should protect and guard the Buddha dharma in this Jambudvipa where 1,000 buddhas come to bless the sentient beings. In reply to that the great king of Kumbhandas promised to protect and guard the Jambudvipa in the southern direction.

His body is red in colour. He shows a wrathful appearance. His right hand holds a sword. His left hand rests on his knee. In Nepalese tradition he is called Khadgaraja and can be seen in the corner of the roof of the temple and also in the entrance of the monasteries.

Virupaksha

Virupaksha is one of the four great kings, who rule the first heaven of desire realm in the west. He is the lord of Nagas. He serves as the guardian of this Jambudvipa of the western direction.

His body is red in colour. He shows a wrathful appearance. His right hand holds a spear of three points; his left fist rests on his knee. He can be recognized through the Caitya symbol in his left hand.

Virupaksha lives in the city of Sudarsana on the west of Sumeru Mountains. His city is as beautiful as that of the three other kings. He leads immeasurable serpent deities i.e. nagas to protect Buddha dharma in the west.

Virupaksha leads besides the retinue of nagas, innumerable spirits of sun and moon and others. They are all responsible for the protection of the Buddha dharma. Devotees worship these four maharajas in a group.

Vaisravana

He is also one of the four great kings who rule the first heaven of the desire realm in the north. He is the lord of Yakshas. Some regard him as also the lord of wealth who gives blessings for prosperity. Sumeru Mountain, supremely beautiful adorned with precious jewels. It is said that his city is as beautiful as Sukhavati heaven in the west. He has five princes and has 28 messengers under his command. They are his retinue.

Like the three other kings, he was also instructed by Buddha Shakyamuni to protect the Buddha dharma in Jambudvipa in the northern direction.

In Nepalese Buddhist tradition Vaisravana or kubera is worshipped singly and is very popular. Newar Buddhists women make the image of Vaishravan out of rice flour during Yomari-Punhi festival (December-January). It is also customary to keep an image of Vaishravan in the treasury room or inside the treasure box.

The worshipping of four guardian deities was introduced in China by Pandit Amogh Vajra during eight century.

Eight Dikpalas (Eight Deities of Direction)

Indra or Sakra

Indra is the king of devas in the heaven of Trayatrimsa or third heaven of the desire realm. He rides on the Airavata elephant and is yellow in colour. He holds in his two hands a vajra and a breast of a woman. He is sometimes seated on the Airavata elephant wearing a headdress. Sometimes with his right hand he holds a Vajra and his left hand rests on a hip. Sakra is a very popular deva in both Hindu and Buddhist tradition.

In the past when Indra was a human being he had thirty-three pious friends. Under his leadership they cultivated many virtues by helping the poor, establishing many wells for thirsty people and houses for travelers. By these virtues he attained the state of Indra, the king of devas in the city of Sudarsana ruling over 32 palaces. The other 32 friends became the governors of these 32 palaces.

Trayatrimsa heaven is a very lovely palace with natural beauty. The city is full of lovely damsels called Apsaras. The only suffering that the citizens of this heaven have is to undergo to fight with Asuras at times. Hence after losing there live or at the end of their life span there arises the five signs or omens, which predict their end of life in that heaven. The story of Sakra fighting against Asuras is a very popular literature in Buddhist and Hindu tradition.

Sakra is said to be a guardian of Buddhism. He always requested Buddha Shakyamuni for dharma teachings for the benefit of all sentient beings. He is better treated in Buddhist literature in contrast to Hindu tradition. He usually made a huge offering to Buddhist Sangha.

Once upon a time, one of the friends of Indra went to Avici Hell and suffered a lot. Through repeated requests of Indra, Buddha Shakyamuni delivered the Tantra of Durgatihari sodhana. When Indra himself was about to die, Buddha Shakyamuni delivered and transmitted the dharma door of Aparimita dharani by which the life span of Sakra was extended significantly.

Yama

Yama or Yamaraja is another popular deva sometimes called the King of the Death. He rides on a buffalo. His right hand holds a banner of a human head, and his left hand holds a Tarjani pasa.

Yama is also responsible for ruling over all the Preta realms. The Sanskrit word *'yama'* stands also for twin rulers. It means that the king of the death governs hells as well as ghost realms together with his sister. He himself rules over dead males and his sister being responsible for talking care of dead females. King Yama lives in palace surrounded by cakravala i.e. an iron-chained mountain in the south of Jambudvipa. As he rules over the hells he dues not enjoy the fruits of his meritorious karma. Because in his past lives, he created evil karmic forces and he had to endure the effects of past karma during three periods of time. When he was in suffering, his palace naturally changed into an iron city of burning flame.

According to the version of some legend, it is said that he was originally a king of Vaisali. At one time he happened to he engaged in a bloody war. He wished he were the master of hell and was accordingly reborn as Yama in hell, together with his generals and army.

According to the Tibetan legends, however, Yamantaka, a wrathful manifestation of Manjushree Bodhisattva, subdued the king Yama.

Kuvera

Kuvera is one of the most popular deities of Nepalese Buddhists because of his bestowed of wealth character. He is generally represented as the lord of wealth and guardian of the northern direction. He is deep yellow in color and holds in his two hands a goad and a gada (mace). Sometimes he is represented sitting on a lion with a green mane, holding a banner of victory in the right hand and carrying the mongoose, which vomits a wish-fulfilling gem.

Kuvera's abode is said to be Alaka in the Himalayas, enriched with wealth and abundance. He is always surrounded with yaksha generals and Kinnars. He may have sometimes a third eye also. In the Durgatiparisodhana Tantra, it is stated, Kubera the great king of the Yakshas, bowed before the Lord Shakyamuni Buddha and said: 0 Lord, I together with eighty eight great war generals of the

Yakshas, will persevere in removing every fear of that great being who holds this tantra. I will give wealth and grain in abundance. I will protect his country and provinces, his people, servants, relatives, friends, sons, daughters, wives and the rest. I will take care of his oxen, cows, asses, camels, sheep, elephants, goats and the rest.

He is thus especially invoked for generating wealth and prosperity. There are many legends relating to his role as guardian of all the treasures of the earth and the treasures belonging to the people. Kuvera is worshipped both by the Hindus and Buddhists alike.

Varuna Deva

Varuna Deva is also one of the powerful deities representing the lord of water element. He is generally presented as white in colour. He sits on a Makara. He has the colour of lotus. He holds the invincible noose and a conch in his hands. He is adorned with the serpent's hood over his head.

In Nepalese Buddhist tradition, in the Guru mandala rite the offerings are also made to Varuna deva in the group of eight. i.e. the deities of eight Directions.

It is said in the Guna Karanda Vyuha Sutra, that Varuna emerged from the knees of Arya Avalokiteshvara and instructed that he should protect the sentient beings by bestowing Amrita or nectar or pure water. Being the lord of the underworld, lord of Nagas, he should bestow riches of the underworld to the people and protect the dharma. Avalokiteshvara instructed, 'If you perform Bodhicarya as I mention, you will definitely acquire tremendous merits and will attain Buddhahood in the future'. In reply Varuna Deva promised to act accordingly.

Agni Deva

Agni Deva is also one of the most powerful devas representing the element of fire presiding in the sooth-east corner. He is red in colour and has great radiance. He is seated on a chariot drawn by seven horses. He has seven tongues and three eyes. He holds a ladle and a Kamandalu in his two hands.

In the Nepalese Buddhist tradition, in the Guru mandala rite, offering is also made to this Agni Deva along with other deities.

He is especially worshipped and revered in the fire offering or home Yajna performance.

The Guna Karandavyuha sutra relates that Agni Deva is originated from the navel of Arya Avalokiteshvara. Arya Avalokiteshvara instructed Agni Deva to purify the phenomenal world by the fire offered to him. Accordingly Agni Deva promised then to abide by the instruction.

Vayu Deva

Vayu Deva is also one of the powerful deities representing the air element. He is generally represented as blue in colour. He resides in the northwest corner. He is riding on a chariot drawn by deer. He carries a flag banner in his hands. He is full of motion. He has the colour of smoke. He is the sustenance for the people.

He is worshipped as is the custom in a group of eight deities of direction in the Guru Mandala rite.

The Guna Karandavyuha sutra further states that Vayu deva is originated from the mouth of Arya Avalokiteshvara. Arya Avalokiteshvara instructed Vayu Deva to protect the sentient beings by being vital prana (vayu) and give blessings and inspire the beings to perform meritorious deeds. He was told that if he performed the deeds as mentioned, he would then certainly attain Buddhahood in future. Vayu deva solemnly accepted the blessings with great devotion.

In Durgatiparisodhana Tantra, the Lord of the wind said, "O Lord, I will never cause that great being to be terrified by winds. I will not produce untimely winds. I will provide grains, flowers and fruits and remove all fears."

Isana Deva

Isana Deva (or Mahadeva) is also one of the eight deities of the directions. The word Isana represents the northeast corner. He resides in the northeast direction. He is seated on a chariot drawn by bulls. He is white in colour and holds in his two hands a trident and a kapala. A half moon appears on his matted hair. He is adorned with a sacred thread of a serpent and his body is besmeared with ashes. His throat appears blue. He is naked and has three eyes.

In the Durgatiparisodhana Tantra, the Lord of the all the spirits bowed before the Lord Buddha and said,

"O Lord with regard to that king, prince warrior or brahman, I will guarantee refuge here and beyond, provide protection, tranquility and happiness, immunity to the sword and punishment counteracting and destroying poison, stability of borders, regions and estates. I will provide them with a Vajra enclosure made of Vajra darts, and a Vajra Canopy. I will assist them in needs and give an indication of what is to be done and what not. I will explain through a dream that is auspicious and inauspicious. I will help for every success with no obstruction to the performers of rites."

As usual he is also worshipped in the Guru Mandala rite of Nepalese Buddhist tradition, in a group of eight deities of directions.

Nairrati Deva

He is also one of the eight deities of the directions. He resides in the southwest corner. He is the lord of the goblins or rakshasa called Nairrati. He is blue in colour and rides on a corpse. His two hands hold a sword and a khetaka or Kapala filled with meat. He has a wrathful face with exposed teeth.

In the Durgatiparisodhana Tantra, in the chapter of Mandala of Dikpalas, Nairrati, 'the great lord of the Rakshasas, said this: "O Lord, with regard to the king, prince brahmana, warrior or any other person who hold this tantra, I will not cause diseases, fear of Pretas and Pisacas, fear of Rakshas and others or fear of untimely death. I will always provide them with security, protection and cover."

As usual he is worshipped in the Guru Mandala rite of Nepalese Buddhism, in a group of eight deities of directions.

Guardian Deities

Mahakala

Mahakala is a deity worshipped both by Hindu and Buddhists. He can be seen in the entrance of every Buddhist monastery of Kathmandu valley. He is said to be the protector of doctrine of Buddha Shakyamuni. There are many forms of Mahakala, among them two-armed, four-armed, six-armed and sixteen-armed being the most popular one.

In the Nepalese Buddhist tradition the two-armed form of Mahakala carved in stone is found in large numbers. This two-armed form is described as follows:

His body is dark blue in colour. He looks wrathful bedecked with ornaments of serpents. He wears a garland of severed heads and a crown of five skulls symbolizing the five defilements. His right hand holds Kartri symbolizing that it can cut ego clinging and attachment, and his left hand holds a kapala filled with blood symbolizing the subjugation of evil ones. He wears tiger skin symbolizing the purification of desire. He has three eyes symbolizing his clear comprehension of three times. He looks ferocious against the blazing fire. His mouth is smeared with blood signifying that he is active in eliminating evils.

The characteristic feature of the Protector Mahakala is that he, during war, can protect those relying on him since there is limitless number of retinue of spirits and ghosts under his command who are skillful in battle. He can provide sufficient foods to the needy. Separate temples with Mahakala alone can be found in large number.

It is said that Mahakala is the manifestation of Bodhisattva Avalokiteshvara. From the heart of Arya Avalokiteshvara emerged a dark blue Hung letter, which transformed into the Instantaneous Protector of wisdom. Buddha Amitabha proclaimed thus, "Son of the family, you shall have the strength of the wrathful Yama, Lord of death. You shall have the mountain spirits, the yakshas, the devils and the demonesses as your messengers. You shall embody the great wrathful empowerments of body, speech, mind, qualities and activities of all the Buddhas throughout the three times". Ever since Mahakala has remained as the doctrine Protector of all the Buddha fields.

Ganesh/Ganapati

Ganesh is one of the most popular guardian deities worshipped in Nepal by Hindus and Buddhists alike. Large numbers of independent temples of Ganesh are found in Kathmandu valley. Ganesh is said to be the deity of eliminator of obstacles. To begin any auspicious work or enterprise Nepalese people adore this deity with the hope that they may accomplish their work successfully by averting the obstacles if there be any. The form of Ganesh or Ganapati is described in Sadhanamala and Nispannayogavali.

Ganapati rides on a mouse and is white in colour. He has an elephant face. A snake forms his sacred thread. He is four-armed. In the two right hands he carries a trisula and a laddu i.e. sweet ball and in the two left hands a parasu i.e. axe and a radish.

Ganesh is said to be the son of Shiva and Parvati. It so happened once that Kumara or Kartikeyya challenged Ganesh to circumambulate the world. The winner's prize was to be to be worshipped by the people first. Kartikeyya travelled the world with his vehicle peacock several times and was about to report this to Lord Shiva and Parvati. Ganesh then thinking that he would not be able to circumambulate the world with his tiny vehicle mouse came out with different idea. He began to circumambulate around Lord Shiva and Parvati thrice.

Lord Shiva and Parvati asked the reason for that. Ganesh replied that this triple world was not greater than his parents and circumambulating them, it is thus far more better than circumambulating the triple world. On hearing the wise answer of his son Ganesh, Lord Shiva and Parvati blessed Ganesh that he should be the first deity to be worshipped before any ritual ceremony or auspicious occasion.

Bibliography

Banerjee, Biswonath *Sri kalacakratantraraja*, Calcutta, 1985.

Beyer, Stephen *Magic & ritual in Tibet, The cult of Tara*, Delhi, 1988.

Bhattacharya, Benoytosh, *The Indian Buddhist Iconography*, Second edition Firma K.L. Mukhopadhyaya, Calcutta, 1958.

Bhattacharya, Benoytosh *Sadhanamala* Vol.1 & II. GOS, Nos. 26 & 41, Baroda, 1925-28.

Bhattachatya, Benoytosh *Guhyasamaja Tantra*. GOS, No.53, Baroda, 1931 (ed.).

Bhattacharya, Benoytosh *Nispannayogavali of Abhaya karagupta* GOS, No 109, Baroda, 1949.

Bhattacharya, Benoytosh *Introduction to Buddhist Esoterism*, Oxford University Press, 1932.

Bhattacharya, D.C. *Studies in Buddhist Iconography*, Chandigarh, 1978.

Bhattacharya, D.C. *Tantric Buddhist Iconographic Sources*, Delhi, 1973.

Bhattasali, N.K. *Iconography of Buddhist & Brahmanical Sculptures in the Dacca Museum*. Dacca, 1929.

Clark W.E. *Two Lamaistic Pantheons two* vols. Harvard Yenching Institute, Monograph series, Cambridge, Massachusetts.

Coomaraswamy, A. K. *Elements of Buddhist Iconography*, Delhi, 1979.

Dowman Keith *Masters of Mahamudra*, New York, 1985.

Evans Wentz, W.Y. *Tibetan Book of the Dead*, Oxford University Press, USA 1960.

Foticher, A *Etnde sur L'Iconographique de L'Inde*, vols I & II, Paris, 1900 & 1905.

Getty, A. *The Gods of Northern Buddhism*, New Delhi, 1978.

Gordon, A.K. *Iconography of Tibetan Lamaism*, New Delhi, 1978.

Ghosh Mallar *A Study of Tara - Prajnas of Five Tathagatas & Bhrikuti*, Delhi, 1980.

Halen, H. *Mirrors of the Void*, Helsinki, 1987.

Hazra, K.L. *The Adi-Buddha*, Delhi, 1986.

Heng Ching *Earth Store Bodhisattva Sutra*, Institute of Advanced Study of World Religions, New York, 1973.

Menon, I. & Farrow, G.W. *Hevajratantra*, Delhi, 1983.

Mitra, R.L. *The Sanskrit Buddhist Literature of Nepal*. Sanskrit Pustak Bhandar, Calcutta 1970 (Reprint).

Rangdol Tsele *The Lamp of Mahamudra,* Rangjung Yeshe Publications, Kathmandu, 1988.

Roerich G. *Tibetan Paintings,* Paris, 1925.

Tadeusz Skorupski *The Sarvadurgatiparisodhana tantra,* Delhi, 1983.

Thrangu Rinpoche *Buddha Nature,* Rangjung Yeshe Publications, Kathmandu, 1988.

Templeman David *The Origin of Tara tantra.* LTWA, Dharamsala, 1981.

Tsonkhapa *Tantra in Tibet,* Wisdom of Tibet Scrics-3, London, 1977.

Vairacharya, *Amogb Astottarasata Lokesvara ya parichaya* Nepal Sambat 1099, Kathmandu (1979 A.D.) Newari.

Vajracharya, Manabajra & Warren W. Smith *The Mythological history of Swayambhu,* Avalok Publishers, Kathmandu, 1978.

Index